This is How it Feels

Craig A. Miller

www.ThisisHowitFeels.com

"'Twas grace that taught my heart to fear.

And grace my fears relieved."

-John Newton (1725-1807).

www.ThisIsHowItFeels.com

CONTENTS

ACKNOWLEDGMENTS

To my friends, you know I love you. I could have never made it through without you. At a time when I was so far from home, you helped me stand up on my own.

To my family, you know I'm sorry. I wish we could have grown a stronger tree. Some limbs are bent and some sections dead, but the shade still comforts me. I wouldn't change it for anything- for all the songs that our birds sing. And every fruit that falls gives seed to the truth that this tree will grow for you.

To you, I miss you. Know that I often think of you. And on nights when time stands still, I linger in it with you. Our nights made dreams and dreams made songs. I found a place where I belonged.

And to my God, you tricked me. I thought you were never there for me. But through these eyes that are strained and tired from the pain, I can see...I can see...that you've always been beside me.

www.ThisisHowitFeels.com

It took me three days to recover from my suicide attempt. For three days in the Intensive Care Unit, machines breathed for me, medications balanced my chemistry, and wired electrodes monitored every vital bodily function imaginable. For three days, family members held their breath while doctors gave word that I may not make it and prepared them for the possibility of permanent brain damage. My mother staggered through the halls of the hospital as the thought of losing her son weakened her steps. My father visited countless times each day, unable to stay long enough to battle the anxiety of helplessness. My two brothers leaned against each other, bracing for the worst possible outcome. And the rest of the world moved on without me.

I was only twenty years old and already felt as though I had lived a hundred lives. From the moment my life began I found myself buried in emotions that dragged me so deep beneath their surface, I could touch the bottom, each time fighting a battle to rise and continue. I had a profound trust that there was purpose and reason for all things, and I used it to continue on a road of life on which I had little control. I believed in God before I was ever introduced, and I always thought of heaven as home. A spark within me dimly lit my way, and I held it dear to my heart. I fought and I fought, and still the war waged on. But then I was done. It was over. I had fought the battles of my life tirelessly. I had given my blood, cried my tears, and worn the scars from a lifetime of struggle, yet the war was lost. I had surrendered.

For most of the time I lay in a comatose-like state, seemingly unresponsive and unaware. But there were brief moments where I would break free and awaken to life. Heart monitors raced and alarms sounded as I suddenly convulsed into spasms of involuntary reflex, as if someone were grinding the ignition of an old car while the alternator burned and the engine desperately shook to turn over. My body begged for life. But my soul stood undecided on the threshold of existence, weighing the balance of all the reasons I wanted to die against the lack of reasons I wanted to live. One by one, my senses exploded outward and reached for any sign of life to hold on to. Lights became intensely bright, sounds amplified, and pain flared.

And then all was still. I was out again, unconscious and unaware. Time moved on without me until suddenly I was again pulled back into reality. Over and over, in and out, and each time I awoke with more clarity and awareness than before. Each time another one of my senses peaked to its highest potential, as if my body were running a diagnostic check on all systems. And between each burst of awakening, I saw my entire life play out before me. Sometimes as still-shot memories and flashes of single moments saturated with feeling. Other times I saw an entire scene that rolled along in a linear dream and allowed me to relive each one.

I lay in a hospital bed for three days while my body sporadically burst to life in brief moments of awareness. But in the moments when I appeared a lifeless body teetering on the edge of death, unconscious and unaware...it was then that I lived like I never had before.

1 THE END

It was a Friday when I decided to kill myself. I had no specific reason for choosing that Friday. It wasn't a bad day or even a bad week. It simply felt like the right time for me. At twenty-years-old, I arrived home that night in the usual way: quiet and withdrawn. My father sat in the living room and welcomed me with a nod as I passed between him and the nightly news. I went into the kitchen and made myself a full pitcher of cherry Kool-Aid. I mixed it in slow circles, counting each revolution, one two three four five. Five is a good number, five times in one direction, five feels right. I stood alone, mixing the foaming red water while it swirled into a deepening center, and for a moment it appeared beautiful. Not in its color or its pirouetting dance but in its purpose. It was smooth, easy to drink, and made to a lukewarm temperature from the faucet so it wouldn't chill my throat on the way down. It was perfect and it had reason.

I took the pitcher up the stairs, where for the last several months I had been renting a room from my father's girlfriend. My father had been living with her for years, and since the state required me to have a permanent address to collect a disability check, they let me stay there as long I agreed to give them a share of it.

They gave me a bedroom on the second floor that came with a beat up old mattress and a dilapidated bureau with missing handles and broken glides. A torn, yellowed shade hung from a cracked window that filtered my view of the gray, cluttered city. There was no heat at that end of the house, and the crack in the window had made the winter months especially cold. At times, I watched my breath circle out in front of me as I fell asleep. But it was summer now, and the pouring rain outside reminded me of how cold the house still felt.

My fingers traced the molding along the edge of the wall in the darkened hallway. All was quiet with only the sound of the fluttering window shade as the city wind tried to pry its way through the crack in the glass. I reached out to open the door, my fingers spread evenly apart to symbolize balance and perfection. My palm, the first part to touch the doorknob, pressed against the hard metal surface. Each finger bent in unison at the first set of knuckles.

Keep them together. They must touch all at the same time.

My body tingled, as though a thin veil of silk had dragged over me. *I must get this right. It must be perfect. Do not make a mistake tonight.* Each finger did as was intended. They worked as one. A slow, methodical sigh escaped my lungs, and relieved the pressure of possible failure.

I went inside, closed the door, and locked myself in the rented room. I set the pitcher of Kool-Aid down on a nightstand made of milk crates. Lined up along its edge were bottles of pills that I had accumulated over the last few months. Pills meant to help control my fears, my emotions, and my thoughts; pills that I had quietly stopped taking because they had never done a thing for me. But now they were about to do everything for me.

I sat on the edge of the bed and placed my most prized

possession in my lap: a black notebook with a faded cover and ragged edges. I slowly turned through it, skimming over lines of poetic verses, paragraphs of thought, and single phrases of personal insight, all written on tear-stained pages in a desperate plea for some kind of peace. I had no need to read it. I knew each page by heart, every word, every phrase, and every syllable. But I had one last verse that needed to escape, a culmination of words that wandered aimlessly through my mind and begged me to help them find a home on a page. With a black pen, a shaking hand, and scarred knuckles, I set them free.

When I cross this bridge let it burn
Let the embers fade from sight
And all the dreams I had not return
To their home inside my mind

Raise the white flag to its place
So they know I lost the fight
But let the scars I have never fade
So at least they'll know I tried

I closed the book, set down the pen, and reached for the bottles of pills. I poured out each one, spreading them out in piles across the cover of my notebook. I began meticulously sorting them into organized groups. One pill at a time, I lined them up according to size and color. They had to be perfect. If this was to go well, then everything must be in good order. Each pill lined up straight and touching another as if they were becoming one. I pressed my finger lightly on top of them as I slowly counted them out one at a time. Two hundred and fifty pills exactly. I knew what they were going to do to me, what purpose they would serve, and how powerfully devastating they would be when taken together. But in that moment they looked so innocent, just soft shapes, laid out harmlessly in colorful groups.

It was one of the most calm and peaceful moments of my entire life. I believed in my heart that it was all going to be over: the worry, the internal battles, the hopelessness, and the crushing fear. No longer would I suffer. No longer would I be alone. I believed in God. I believed in eternity. I knew where I was going.

I placed the pills in my hand one group at a time and swallowed them with the entire pitcher of Kool-Aid. I held the notebook against my chest with both arms, laid back on the rented bed, and rested my head on a borrowed pillow. My eyes were sore. They were tired and worn from the years of emotion that had forced my tears to fall. My chest ached. It held a broken heart that struggled to beat despite the scars that crippled it. And my head throbbed. It smoldered like a battlefield where the enlightening dreams of hope had fought against the darkness of disillusioned thoughts.

I took a deep breath and whispered into the night, "God, please let me come home." My body weakened, and I fell into a dizzying darkness.

2 THE FEAR

I woke on a cold Saturday morning to a fresh layer of New England snow that blanketed the neighborhood outside my window. My three-year-old imagination spun with excitement as I peered in awe through a pane of glass that separated me from a winter wonderland that lay just beyond my reach. I had an infatuation with playing in a new, undisturbed snow fall. Nothing compared to the feeling of running through it, kicking up the light powder, and making my own path of footprints across a smooth, blank canvas of white. I pretended that it was all mine and had fallen just for me. But my excitement quickly turned to disappointment when I realized that it was only six in the morning. There was no way I would get permission to go outside. Waking my mother at this hour was forbidden, especially on a Saturday.

My parents had divorced when I was a year old. My mother got to keep me, her two sons from a previous marriage, and the house my father bought. It was a small, box-shaped house, located just far enough away from the city's busy downtown area to give the illusion of a safe rural setting. Our neighborhood was tightly packed with a mix of single-family homes and multi-level apartment houses all crammed together along narrow streets. Neglected fences separated yards and driveways while bushes grew wildly out of control, serving as the only form of privacy.

The inside of our house was just as tight as the neighborhood outside. I was lucky enough to have my own bedroom while my two half-brothers shared a room off the kitchen. They were close in age to each other but nearly a decade older than me, and most people wouldn't believe we were brothers. They had thick black hair, deep brown eyes and strong builds. My hair was almost white-blond. I was small with a fragile frame, and my eyes were an innocent shade of green. My mother had married when she was sixteen and gave birth to them both right away. Their father ran out on them shortly after, and he never looked back. My mother quickly remarried. I was born, and the cycle continued. Now she was on her third marriage, this time to Jake.

Jake was a hardcore cowboy from Texas and had a stern face that looked bulletproof. He rarely spoke with my brothers and me. More than anything, he was just a guy who lived there with us. The only time he made his presence known was when he and my mother were fighting. Their relationship was volatile and often exploded into screaming matches that ended with flying fists and broken furniture. Most of the time the battles were on a Friday or Saturday night, which is why it was so important to never wake her up early on the weekends. She was typically a hung-over emotional wreck, and I had learned the hard way how critical it was to keep quiet. I would get up in the morning and lie underneath our coffee table, eating cereal from the box and watching Saturday morning cartoons with the volume off.

But on that day, Saturday morning cartoons were just going to have to wait. The smooth bed of snow outside my window was more than I could bear. I pressed my forehead against the cold glass to try and see into the neighborhood in front of our house. That was where I wanted to go. Nothing had been shoveled or plowed yet. The undisturbed layer of white hid the contrast of the street and sidewalks. Our compact neighborhood looked like one giant field of snow to my wide three-year-old eyes.

I knew that my mother would not be awake until one or two in the afternoon and she would still need at least another hour to adjust to the day. Only then would it be safe enough to talk to her and ask to go outside. But I couldn't wait that long. I had to go now.

I quietly searched my bedroom for clothes, rummaging through piles of laundry and scattered toys that covered the floor. I put my pants on over my pajamas and slipped on a pair of green rubber boots. All I needed was my jacket, but that was complicated. I had yet to perfect how to put it on properly. The only way I knew how was to lay it on the floor and put my arms into each sleeve then stand up and flip it over my head. Knowing it was a noisy process that involved some complex moves, I decided to take it with me and wrestle with it outside.

I tiptoed into the kitchen being extra careful as I passed by my mother's closed bedroom door. I used a kitchen chair to reach the deadbolt, slowly sliding it across the floor so it didn't make a sound. I opened the door, cautious not to let any of the house's heat escape with me, and I stepped out into the frigid New England air.

The rising sun glimmered off the snow. My eyes widened with the wonder of playing in it. I laid the jacket on the ground and did my best to remember the arm-flip trick but struggled over and over as I continued to somehow end up wearing it upside-down. After a half-dozen tries I gave up; the jacket was staying upside down. I didn't care. I wanted to get to that snow. I imagined throwing it up in the air and letting it fall all around me like a real-life snow globe.

A white picket fence surrounded our tiny yard and stood as the only barrier between me and a day full of fun on the other side of the its locked gate. But the latch on the gate was complicated with turns, bends, and slides. So I bypassed the gate, and climbed up the snow banking that was formed from shoveling our walkway after previous storms.

I planted my feet at the top of the banking, struggling to keep my balance in the soft mountain of snow, and nervously looked down at the height of my drop to the other side of the fence. I shuffled and twisted my feet at the top of the mound. Hunched down, bent at the knees, I prepared to spring back up and make the leap over the top of the fence. I jumped up, but things didn't go as planned. As I pushed off, my feet sank into the soft snow, and my momentous leap became a stumbling nosedive.

My shins scraped against the top of the pickets. I braced for a hard face-first landing, but my pant leg caught on one of the picket points. My body swung downward like a broken tree branch that was still attached to the trunk. My head scraped into a whitewash of snow while my ankle stayed twisted at the top of the fence.

There was nothing I could do. I hung helplessly upside down from a picket fence with my head buried in the snow. I wiggled and squirmed but it was no use. I knew I was never getting down on my own. My mind fought to determine what would be worse: the blood rushing to the top of my frozen head or my mother's early morning hangover?

I shook with one last attempt to get off the fence, but it was hopeless. The pant leg supporting all my weight twisted around my ankle, cutting off the circulation to my foot. It burned with pain and froze in the winter air. Hysteria took over. My entire leg was going to break off or I was going to freeze to death without anyone ever finding me. My head throbbed with the blood that was now settling in my brain, and I screamed out.

I yelled and cried, calling for my mother in between wails. I screamed over and over for what felt like hours, falling deeper into fright as my foot numbed, and my head inflated with pressure.

Suddenly, the front door swung open with such force, the air whistled around it. "What the hell are you doing?" my mother yelled.

I knew from her tone that she was angry.

"I'm... stuck... Mom...I...can't... get... down." My words squeezed out between deep wails of panic.

"Damn it all!" she yelled before going back inside and slamming the door shut again.

I knew I was in trouble. I was outside without permission, and it was way too early for my mother to be up. She was inside for what felt like forever. I could hear her yelling from inside the house. "Son of a bitch! I'm not going out there and getting him."

I worried she would leave me hanging to die in the snow.

"The only Goddamn day I get to sleep and I got to do this shit. Get up and go get your brother." Her voice sounded like claps of distant thunder to my frozen ears and pounding head.

The door swung open again, and my oldest brother Jay

came running out in pajamas and boots. He and my other brother, Tyler, were seasoned veterans when it came to our mother's wrath.

"Don't worry, Craig, I'm going to get you down from there," he said as he frantically worked to unhook me from the fence. "Just stop moving, will ya?" Jay was a tough kid with a strong streetwise attitude. He had a chiseled face and a chipped front tooth that let you know he wasn't afraid to take a punch. He had been through a lot with my mother and her husbands over the years. He had lived through the worst of the poverty, the emotional instability, and the abuse. Everyone has their own way of adapting, and Jay's was to put up his fists, grow up fast, and harden his shell.

He lifted me and untwisted my pant leg to free me from the picket. It felt like my ankle was going to snap and I screamed in pain. My mother stood in the doorway yelling at us. "Get him in here, Jay. Hurry Up! I'm not going to stand here all Goddamn day."

Jay turned me upright and helped me to gain my balance. He knelt, brushing the snow off my face and shoulders. "You're okay. You're okay." he said, while I continued wailing. "What the hell are you doing out here? Are you crazy?"

"I just wanted to play." I tried to calm myself. Crying was only going to make my mother angrier. "I didn't want to wake Mom up." My voice shook through the sobs. I tried to catch my breath and adjust to the dizziness that was making me top-heavy as Jay helped me limp back into the house. My mother stood waiting in the doorway.

"What the hell is wrong with you?" my mother snapped.

"I didn't want to wake you up."

"You just couldn't wait, could you? Goddamn it, Craig! The only time I get to fucking sleep, and you have to pull this shit? Jesus Christ!"

Jay pulled my arms from the upside-down jacket and tried to help me calm down. "Don't worry, Craig. Look at me." He moved his face in front of mine to try and break me from my fearful trance. "Don't worry about Mom, okay? Just relax."

My mother's temper had little effect on Jay. She had gotten angry at him so many times over the years that he could easily shut her out.

I shivered violently from the cold. My cheeks felt raw, and my eyes were streaming tears. The muscles around my jaw ached with the intense strain of my sobs, and my lungs burned.

"Don't worry about her." Jay's voice was barely discernible through the sounds of my mother's tirade. I shook, awaiting the outcome of her unpredictable anger, while she walked through the house with heavy steps slamming the doors and yelling about all the problems I had caused. When she came back into the kitchen, she sent Jay to his room.

"What the hell were you doing outside?" she asked again. Her hot breath plumed in my face with the smell of scotch and stale cigarettes. Even in her angriest moments, she had never hit me. I had no reason to believe that she would do it this time, but my body still braced for impact.

"I just wanted to play in the snow," I answered quietly.

"This is bullshit! You want to play in the Goddamn snow at this hour of the morning? Are you fucking kidding me?" She took my arm and led me back to my room. I tried to keep up with her pace while my ankle throbbed.

"You know what? That's it, you blew it. You want to play in the snow? Tough shit!" She let me go with a shove, and I caught my balance on the edge of the bed.

I looked over at the window. The brilliant white light of the reflective snow looked like a portal to another dimension in the dim light of my room.

"I had enough of this shit," she continued. "No snow for you. You're not going anywhere. You're not leaving your room, and you are definitely not going outside."

She reached up and pulled down the window shade as if she were slamming a metal barricade. The soft winter morning vanished behind its veil, darkening my room. The only light left was from a small lamp that I kept on to help me sleep.

"You can sit and think about what you've done." She swiped the light switch with a quick downward motion as if she was trying to break it off the wall. She left, slamming the bedroom door shut. My room went completely black. I lay on the bed, sobbing alone in the dark and separated from the world outside.

+++++

The air around me seemed to thicken. Dizziness swept through my head with an amazing force. My sobs continued, constricted my lungs. I suddenly couldn't breathe. *I wanted to call for my mother. I needed help, but I couldn't make a sound. I couldn't move. My muscles felt paralyzed. I lay motionless while I felt the sensation of my bed lifting, shaking, and rattling.*

My mother's distant rant twisted and warped. It overlapped with other voices. They blended together, yelling over one another, until they were all drowned out by the sound of a screaming siren. I lay breathless, in a dizzying confusion, gripped by the dark loneliness, as the howling sounds of the siren faded away.

3 THE MESSAGE

I pulled my knees into my chest and buried my head in a pillow wet with tears. The walls were shaking, windows were rattling, and doors were slamming. She was angry again, and there was nothing- not even the concern for her six-year-old son- that could deter her from her rage. I was used to my mother's anger by now. I had heard her yell and seen her scream through tears, and I had witnessed her storm through our house breaking everything in sight. But this time it was different. This time it was only three days before Christmas.

She and the cowboy had divorced about a year earlier. Their relationship ended in a rampage one night that left the inside of our house unrecognizable. My mother stabbed the water bed and cut it apart, while she screamed about never sleeping with him again. Water ran from her bedroom across the entire living room.

That was the first time I had ever seen a police officer up close. Two of them came to the house that night around midnight. Broken lamps left the house dark. The lights from police cars came through the windows and lit our living room with flashes of blue. Both cops came in through the front door, shining flashlights around, sloshing through the water-logged shag carpet and stepping over debris. My mother held me on her hip. I squeezed my arms around her, sobbing, scared to death that the men with guns were going to take my mother away.

One of the cops wanted to arrest her, but the other one talked him out of it. "We can't take her in. Look at the little one here." He pointed to me.

After that night the police never returned, and neither did my mother's husband.

But now she was with Steve. Up to this point all of her relationships had been brief bouts of unhealthy battles that were destined to end in all-out war. Her relationship with Steve was different, despite not being much better than any of her last. They fought just as violently as she had with all her other husbands and boyfriends, but Steve wasn't a natural fighter- not like the other guys and not like my mother. He certainly stuck up for himself, but it was clear that he wasn't used to my mother's intense mood swings. Her idea of a relationship was to fight like you never wanted to see the other person again, then make up like you had just fallen in love. It was a pattern I had seen many times. But this time her sparring partner wasn't playing along as easily. And despite the chaos, Steve stuck around. It could have been because he was more reserved than the others... on the surface, anyway. As my mother would say, "he walks softly but carries a big stick."

He let her get away with a lot, not saying much until he had finally had enough. Then she got the fight she was looking for. When it boiled down to it, they were the perfect match. My mother loved the opportunity to let the worst of herself come out, and Steve loved the opportunity to try and tame the wild, unpredictable woman she was. Steve became an anomaly in her eyes. She loved him more than anyone else and thought he was perfect. But I didn't.

He was another cowboy type, divorced with three kids of his own. I had a very hard time adjusting to him. He was extremely demanding of my mother's attention and didn't like anyone getting in the way of that. He shared her opinion that kids were a burden rather than a part of the family, and he drove a wedge between me and her to ensure he was put first. His jealousy went far beyond just me. It was widespread, and my mother's flirtatious nature was always an issue. And on that night, just days before Christmas, things had escalated beyond control. Steve had had enough, and my mother got the fight she was looking for.

We had just gotten home a couple hours before from a Christmas party at their friend's house. They had a bar set up in a finished basement lit with colored Christmas lights that were strung all around the room. Bowls of spiked eggnog and punch were laid out across a buffet table, while the sounds of whirling blenders and outdated Christmas music filled the gaps in conversation.

Most of the people there were friends of friends or coworkers: just about everyone who had no other place to go for Christmas. It was always easy to pick out the people who were there as part of a matchmaking scheme. The night started off with awkward flirtatious conversations and ended with drunken women wearing Santa hats and carrying mistletoe. My mother was a Santa-hat-and-mistletoe kind of girl, dancing around the room rubbing against other men while spilling scotch down the sides of her glass.

Steve's jealousy got the best of him that night, but he kept it in until we got home. He and my mother were now having one of their drunken screaming bouts and throwing painful one-liners at each other in an attempt to see who could out-hurt the other. Steve's big weapon was criticizing my mother's weight. It was something she battled with her whole life. She wasn't obese by any means; she was just very sensitive about her appearance. Once he threw out a derogatory remark aimed at her self-esteem, I knew the growing tension would turn into something serious. And on this night, as I lay curled up beneath my covers, the fighting was the worst I had ever seen.

For hours she stormed through the house screaming in a scotch-fueled tirade while tears and black eyeliner streaked down her face. On some level, I think she enjoyed these times. Fighting was the fuel for her well-tuned anger-engine. It gave her the release she needed and the justification to lose her mind and self destruct.

She stood in the kitchen, took one glass at a time from the cabinet, and smashed it against the wall until the cabinet was empty. She pulled drawers of silverware from their glides and threw them across the room. I cowered in my bed as each drawer broke apart with a piercing metallic ring. Steve yelled back at her with a low, fiery growl, and smashed his fist into the walls around him. The exchanges of their hateful words were only drowned out by the cracks and smashes of destruction while they worked to outdo each other's rage. Each punch to the wall and thrown object shook our old, fragile house to the core.

I wrapped my arms tightly around a stuffed Winnie the Pooh beneath my covers and pressed my hands together. "Please God, protect the Christmas tree. Please don't let them hurt the presents."

It had been somewhat of a tradition in our house to put all the presents under the tree early. We never had much money, so Christmas was always a big deal at our house. My mom would separate each gift and wrap the pieces individually so it looked like we were getting more than we really were. She strategically placed them under the tree putting the largest ones in back and sizing them accordingly to the front. It helped us forget that we didn't have much money on Christmas.

Another crack of destructive thunder shook the house. My cheek pressed hard against the warm wet surface of my pillow. "Please God, make them stop. Don't let them hurt the tree," I whispered again through my cries.

The light from our Christmas tree shone through the small opening in my bedroom door, and I caught the highlights of a painting that hung on my wall. It was a crude depiction of Christ on a black velvet canvas. My father had hung it on my wall back when I was too young to remember, back when he and my mother we still together. It was a profound image yet it lacked detail, as though the entire thing was done with a steel putty knife. A single shade of beige made up the body of a man stretched out over the outline of a cross. Crimson streaks applied with a fingertip told the story of pain, faith, and trust. And behind it all was a bright shining sun that burst outward in all directions with shades of yellow, gold, and white. The image itself had taught me everything I knew of God at that time: that if I believed, then I would be saved. And at six years old, as I lay in my bed shaking and flinching with every crash of broken glass and flying fist, I imagined He was staring back at me through the black velvet canvas, waiting for me to believe.

I was too scared to move, but I had to. I had to get closer to the painting. I had to ask God why this was happening, why I lived in a house with so much anger and why my mother and a man I barely knew were breaking it apart again. I had to beg God to make it stop. I had to let Him know I was here and that I believed in Him. I held my breath, set Winnie the Pooh to the side and tossed open my covers.

I ran over to my school backpack on my bedroom floor and frantically looked for a piece of paper and something to write with. Shadows of flying objects broke through the stream of Christmas tree light that barely lit my room. I found what I needed and began to quickly scribble.

Deer God,

Please tell me wy this is hapaning. I promis I beleve in you. write me back. I love you!

I crunched the words together tight and wrote as small as I could, leaving enough room for Him to write his reply.

Outside my door the TV flew from its stand and crashed on the floor with a powerful thud that I felt in my stomach. The couch overturned as cushions scattered. Lamps blew out sparks from their sockets as they were ripped from the wall, and the coffee table tore jagged lines through the drop ceiling as Steve launched it across the room. The sounds of screaming, crying, and thunderous crashes contaminated our house.

I climbed on top of a plastic toy box, folded the note, and reached up to the black velvet portal to heaven. The canvas shook against my wall with the vibrations on the other side. I pulled the bottom of the painting away from the wall and slipped the note behind it into the space between the frame and canvas. "Please make it stop," I whispered under my breath as I moved quickly back into bed. I pulled the sheets back up and squeezed Winnie the Pooh.

Through the small opening in my bedroom door, I saw my mother kicking her way through our presents. "You want to ruin my fucking Christmas?" she screamed. Her voice raw and dry, her hair a mess and her face covered in smears of black. "Fuck you. I'll fucking ruin Christmas, you son of a bitch!"

She reached out with both hands and tore at the tree in the corner of the living room. The branches broke apart by the strings of lights that stretched to the wall sockets. And in the midst of my cries, with my arms wrapped around a stuffed Winnie the Pooh and my hands folded in front of me, I watched our Christmas tree fly across the room and crash to the floor in an explosion of red, gold, and green.

"God, no!" I buried my head in my wet pillow and

closed my eyes to the shimmering silver of tinsel slowly floating in the air while the tirade continued into the night.

I woke the next morning and opened my bedroom door to devastation. Everything was broken. Pictures hung crooked on the walls in cracked glass frames, broken furniture and torn-up presents littered the floor, and our Christmas tree lay on its side. At my feet was an ornament I had made for my mother at school: a plastic spoon with red construction paper cut in the shape of Santa Claus and cotton balls glued together forming a billowy white beard. On the back was written "Merry Christmas, Mom."

I had cried so much the night before, I had nothing left. I carefully looked around the house, stepping over broken glass and pieces of what used to be our furniture. For some reason, despite the incredible mix of emotions that flowed through me, I was overcome with the need to absorb the moment. I stood calm and quiet, paying attention to all I felt: the devastation, the anger, the broken spirit, and the loneliness. How could they do this? This was our home. These were our things. This is where we are supposed to be safe. And my own mother, along with a man I barely knew, destroyed it...again... on Christmas.

I walked back to my room, closed the door, and climbed onto my toy box. I pulled the note from the back of the black-velvet painting and unfolded it. My heart beat heavily. I wondered what God had written. But when I opened it, the space I had left for Him to write me back was blank. There wasn't a single letter or even a marking, not even a hint that he was there. Why didn't he write me back? Did I do something wrong? Did I make Him mad? My stomach sank. I realized I had made several spelling errors. It was my fault. God was disappointed in me for not making the words perfect. He was mad that I misspelled a letter to Him.

But as that thought entered my mind, the need to absorb the moment came over me again. This feeling somehow separated me from the pain and sadness I felt for our demolished house and the confusion I felt for the letter. It made it seem as though I was looking at it all from an outside perspective. And I was told to relax and just pay attention.

Something profound came over me. Without thinking, without knowing what it meant, and without consciously making the decision to do it, I laid the note on the floor, picked up a blue magic marker, and wrote in the empty space on the note in big bold letters: *DON'T EVER FORGET HOW THIS FEELS.*

A wave of peace came over me like a reassuring blanket that warmed the cold-hearted air of that morning. I didn't know where the source of that inspiration to write came from, but what I did know is that in that moment, as our home lay in broken pieces and my heart fell heavy with confusion and sadness, I felt as though I wasn't alone and that somehow there was a reason for absolutely everything.

+++++

My vision blurred as the image of the paper and our demolished house waved in front of me like a thin veil of light. A deep darkness set in, and the sounds of unfamiliar voices filled the air around me. They spoke quickly. Their tone bordered on desperation. An energy of panic and heart-stopping concern vibrated around me. But despite the unsettling darkness, the frantic-unfamiliar voices, and the aura of panic, I felt calm. The peaceful, profound moment of receiving that message had become part of me and settled in my core: pay attention, there is a reason for everything, and it will be okay.

My awareness seemed to float, caught in the midst of a dreamlike state. I saw only darkness and heard the voices fading as they continued to frantically call out commands.

4 THE WEB

I knelt down and hunched over a small area of dirt I had dug up in the yard. A magnifying glass in my hand waved across the surface while my fingers sifted and shook the loose soil below. I closed one eye to get a better look and wiped my forehead as if the heat of the Egyptian desert sun were cooking me alive. I had just gotten home from an *Indiana Jones* movie, and the thought of being an ancient Egyptian explorer danced in my six-year-old imagination.

"Wud you doin?" Ben asked from behind me.

"I'm looking for treasures," I said.

"Kie play?"

"Yeah, but don't step on anything," I said. "You have to be careful."

Ben was a tall, mentally challenged man in his early twenties. He was mostly deaf and spoke with a loose tone that made his words blend into awkward syllables. The two hearing aids he wore barely helped him enough to get by, so our communication was difficult at times.

"Just be careful, Ben," I said again, making sure he heard me.

"I wiw."

He knelt next to me to look through the dirt, and I was hit with the pungent smell of Lysol and cat urine that forced me to wince. Ben lived down the street with his grandmother, known by most as the "Cat Lady." Their house was a run-down single-family with a cat in nearly every window. I had been inside with him a few times, and the smell always knocked me over. The house was like nothing I had ever seen before. Cobwebs lined the corners of each room where the ceilings met the walls. Debris and cat hair lay scattered over a musty-brown carpet. Its fibers flattened to a black sheen from years of trampling. Huge piles of dirty laundry scattered across the floor and flopped over the furniture. There were stacks of paper plates everywhere, dried hard with rotting cat food. But what made it look even worse than it was were the windows. The glass panes were covered in a murky film. Some windows had no curtains or shades but the film was so thick it obscured any view inside or out.

Ben and I went inside the house once to fill up water balloons. The dishes were stacked so high in the sink, we couldn't use the faucet. Ben pulled some of them away and found maggots crawling across a stack of dinner plates. Ben's grandmother emptied a can of Lysol on them while they squirmed and dropped in the sink. I rarely went back inside after that, but the smell of the house was burned in my nose. Every time Ben and I played together it always seemed to linger in the air around him.

I politely moved over to avoid the distraction and continued peering through my magnifying glass.

"Do you find it?" Ben asked.

"Not yet. We need to keep looking."

"Okay." His expression showed his extraordinary patience. He was content with doing just about anything and he never complained or got frustrated. We often played a game called "trains." He was the engine, and I was the cargo. He would spend hours pulling me around the neighborhood in a little Radio Flyer wagon, never getting tired and never asking to stop. He had a fascination with mechanics and would stand at the edge of a neighbor's lawn for hours if he saw them out mowing the grass. He never spoke to them and never got in the way. Most of the older people were used to him. They had known Ben since he was born and had the last twenty-something years to get used to him. But it wasn't like that with newer people, especially the families with kids my age.

Ben's disabilities certainly made him stand out, but what made most people uncomfortable were his appearance and mannerisms. He was tall and lanky and walked with a knock-kneed gait, keeping his head cocked to the side like a confused dog. He stared at the ground and had a disturbing habit of picking at his eyebrows and eyelashes until no hair was left and his skin was raw. His thick black hair stood in all directions on his head with small flakes of dandruff that sometimes speckled his shoulders. He wore long tube socks with mismatched stripes that he kept pulled up to his knees, and low-cut sneakers that were always too tightly laced with big loops that flopped around when he walked. His face was covered in neglected pimples, and a thin, see-through mustache lined his upper lip which hung loose as if he were about to drink from an invisible straw.

It was this that made most of the newer families dismiss him when he stood peering over their shoulders working on cars. But to me, he was just an overgrown kid. He was innocent and didn't know any better, and, like me, he had nobody else to play with.

With the wolf-pack mentality of young kids, any weakness is spotted in an instant. Once you show it, you are marked forever. I was quiet and self-conscious, and I had been afraid of my own shadow for as long as I could remember. That was all it took to set the social stage for me. I was on my own, isolated from the other kids. But Ben didn't judge me. He didn't pick on me, and he didn't call me names. Instead, he pulled me around in my wagon and helped me make water balloons. He stood outside my window every morning in the summer waiting for me to come out and play. And he sat next to me while I looked for diamonds in the dirt.

"I think I got one!" I said with excitement pulling a gray stone from the ground. "Aw, it's just a rock."

"A rock, yeah, just rock," Ben mimicked.

"Let's look somewhere else." I got back on my feet and brushed the dirt off my knees.

I made my way around the yard, creeping through the tight space between our shed and the stockade fence that surrounded it, pretending it was a chiseled-out tunnel in an Egyptian pyramid. Ben quietly followed. We continued around the back of the house to a small, crudely built wooden door that hung on rusted hinges. It led to a dark, dirty crawl space beneath a section of the house. *What a perfect place to explore,* I thought!

I opened the rusted latch and slowly swung it open like I was breaking into the entrance of a king's tomb. Cobwebs stretched with the door and the smell of moldy wood and stale air rushed from the darkness like it had been waiting years to escape. The light from the sun beamed a yellow path through the dark that sparkled with tiny specs of reflective dust. I hesitated. I remembered my mother telling me to stay out of there. But if we were quiet, she wouldn't know. I carefully knelt down to crawl inside, holding back a cough as the musty air filled my nose and throat.

The crawl space was tight, only about two-and-a-half feet tall. The dirt floor and stacks of stones that made up our house's foundation made it seem like a secret mystical cave. Ben followed, crouching to fit through the small space. His height and size made it much harder for him to fit, but he played along perfectly, keeping quiet and following my slow movements. He closed the door behind us, carelessly disregarding his own strength, and it thumped like a kick to a loud bass drum. Plumes of dust billowed up in the small beams of sun that broke through the wood panels. The tomb became pitch black.

"*Shh*," I whispered as I pointed to the ceiling. I could hear the footsteps from my family shuffling above and became nervous that I would get in trouble for going in there. "Those are the enemies looking for the same treasure we are. We need to be quiet."

The rays of broken sunlight were just enough to help my eyes adjust to the darkness, and the details of the stone-stacked foundation began to come into view, highlighting the jagged rocks with dark crevasses between them. Spider webs lined the corners and stretched up to the floorboards above us.

I slowly crawled in deeper, my knees dragging across the soft dirt, kicking up the fine dust that had settled over the years. The darkness made it hard to see where we were going, but it gave an authenticity to the tomb that sent my imagination soaring. The dirt floor, the spider webs, and the smell of stale air and dust-- I was a true explorer!

About mid-way through the room, a small beam of light had broken through the door and settled in a circular glow on the floor. "This must be where the treasure is," I whispered, pointing to the small circle of light. My heart raced with anticipation. I could see the grin on Ben's face as my eyes further adjusted to the darkness. He was catching on and beginning to share my excitement in finding the treasure. I used the handle of my magnifying glass and began scratching into the dirt.

"What do you think we'll find?" I whispered.

"Rocks?" Ben asked, seemingly unsure.

"No, diamonds."

"Yeah, diamond," he said, nervously picking at his eyebrow.

I looked down intently, digging through the highlighted glow on the ground and waiting in anticipation to see the shine of a golden coin, the sparkle of a red ruby, or the intense glimmer of a faceted diamond. But I was jolted from my imagination when a huge black spider crawled from the shadows on the floor and crossed the patch of light. Panic hit my stomach. I lost my balance falling backward. The spider disappeared into the shadows. Ben, without even flinching, smiled a wide devious grin and picked feverishly at his eyebrow.

"Hehe, spiders, spiders." He giggled under his breath

in excitement. He had a look on his face that I had never seen before, and it made me nervous. He flapped one hand in front of him almost involuntarily like a leaf in the wind.

"Spiderrrr." He cocked his head and looked off into his own realm.

I had never seen him like this. It was like someone had flipped a switch inside him. He was giddy with excitement but at the same time eerily devious.

"I hate spiders," I said defensively, trying to get him to tame his excitement.

"Spiderrrr," he said, staring at the ground and picking as his eyebrow. "Spider gonna git youw," he said in a strangely playful way, reaching out at me with his hand spread wide and his fingers wiggling, mimicking the legs of a spider.

"Don't tease me." I nervously waved his hand away.

"Spider gonna git youw." He slid closer to me.

"Ben, stop it. You're scaring me."

He laid his hand on the floor with his fingers spread wide and bent sharply. The dark hair on his skin and dried, calloused knuckles made it look like a tarantula in the dimly lit room. His hand crawled across the floor up my arm and onto my shoulder. I dropped the magnifying glass, trying to brush him away, but his mock spider wouldn't move.

"Stop it!" I said in a firm whisper, still trying to keep from being detected by my family above. "I don't like spiders Ben. It's not funny. Get it off me."

He moved closer, his eyes dark and glazed, and his usually expressionless face looked angry and cold. With his hand still contorted he pressed his fingertips into my chest and pushed me hard into the ground. I was stunned by his strength, and I suddenly realized how much older than me- and stronger than me- he really was.

"Dooon't mooove," he said with a hypnotic look on his face. "Spider goona git you." His voice was deep and drawn. He pressed his hand at the base of my throat and drove me flat into the ground. He leaned across me and a wet, pungent armpit pressed into my chest as he locked me down with his elbow on one side and his hip on the other. The rocks in the dirt floor stabbed into my back. I tried to move, but he was too heavy and too strong. My heart pounded, and my stomach turned in a twisted knot. The smell of cat urine, Lysol, and sweat filled the musty room.

"Ben, please get off me." I winced, my eyes filling with tears.

"Spiiiderr," he whispered in a low drone.

The silhouette of his large, lanky body and disheveled hair took on a demonic appearance in the darkness of the room. I felt him pull up my shirt and tiptoe his fingers down the soft skin of my belly.

"Spiiiderr..."

I was frozen in fear. Tears dripped down the sides of my eyes and puddled in my ears. The pressure of his body on my chest and the wave of panic in my heart made it nearly impossible to breathe. His hand trailed across my skin while each finger continued mimicking the legs of a spider pouncing with every step on the way to attack its prey.

"Spiiiderr..."

I imagined the door to the Egyptian tomb opening and a burst of sunlight burning the monster on top of me. I imagined suddenly having magical powers to change him back to the person I knew. And I imagined having the strength to make him stop.

"Please leave me alone," I quietly cried.

With only the silhouette of his back, I couldn't see what he was doing, but I could feel it. I could feel everything: the rocks stabbing into my back, the weight on my chest, the panic in my heart, and the hands that trailed across my body, pulling off the rest of my clothes.

"Spiiiderr gonna bite youw..." The silhouette of his head disappeared into the shadows as he went for my exposed skin.

I lay motionless, too scared to make a sound and too scared to move. Tears dripped down the sides of my face. I watched the dust slowly float through the air and shine like tiny diamonds in a yellow beam of sunlight. Jagged rocks and dark empty spaces lined the walls that surrounded me. And my family's footsteps creaked on the floor above.

In that moment, as I lay beneath my mother's house, hidden from the world behind a thin wooden door and breathlessly panicked in the grip of my frantically beating heart, I closed my eyes, held my breath, and felt the dry, cracked, calloused hands of a man weave a web across a young boy's body.

+++++

The dark corners of the room closed in around me until all light had been consumed. The ground beneath me changed from dirt and rocks to a cold flat surface. My heart still raced with the panic of the moment I had just relived. My eyes. I wanted to open my eyes. I wanted to see, but I was consumed in a deep void of total black. And though I couldn't see anything, I could feel. God, could I still feel. His hands seemed to multiply all over my skin as if four of him gripped me and tore at me. I felt my shirt rip off. I felt my pants tear up each leg. I tried so hard to fight, to get them off of me. I jumped and turned and waved my arms to fight away each hand that covered my body, held my wrists, and pinned my legs. But I couldn't get them off.

"Keep him down!" a woman's voice yelled, cutting through the darkness. Over and over I tried to move, tried to get up, tried to run but the hands held me back. I wanted to yell, I wanted to scream but my voice failed in my breathless hysteria. There were so many hands. I somehow felt I wasn't there anymore, that I wasn't under the house, but I could still smell it. I swear to God, I could still smell it. The dust, the dirt, the Lysol, and cat urine burned in my nose. God get them off me! Leave me alone! Please make them leave me alone.

"Keep his hands back. We need restraints," another voice called out. *My desperate plea to scream and fight was useless, and I felt myself collapsing inward.*

5 THE FIGHT

My feet dragged over the pavement as cold slush and melting snow found its way into my shoes. A green backpack with a picture of the Incredible Hulk on it hung wet and heavy from my shoulders, and my pants stuck to my legs with waterlogged magnetism. Tears streamed down my cold red cheeks while blood dripped over my chapped lips. My palms stung with raw scraped skin, and my nose throbbed with a sensation so strong, it rattled my teeth with every heartbeat. I was seven-years-old and doing everything I could to hold myself together as I staggered home from elementary school, where I had just been beaten up.

I wish I could say that the incident beneath the crawl space of my house was a one-time thing, but it wasn't. The days of Ben pulling me around the yard in a wagon and digging for treasures were slowly being replaced with formidable attacks. I became more and more withdrawn. I kept it all a secret, fearing what might happen to me if I didn't. My reluctance to speak out about it was never based on threats but rather the fear of the unknown. I was scared to death of my mother's unpredictable anger. I worried that my brothers would be ashamed of me for not being strong enough to fight him off. And I was nervous my father would murder a mentally handicapped man who just didn't know any better. Overall, I felt that I was the one to blame and the one to be punished.

Each time the incidents occurred, Ben took them to a new level more heinous than the last. He spent hours standing in front of the crawl space door demonstrating his incredible patience while I continued playing in the yard around him trying to ignore what he was waiting for. When he couldn't lure me inside, he pounced whenever and wherever he could- sometimes in the open space of my own backyard. Other times it happened in his grandmother's basement where we got tools to build forts and bike ramps. Sometimes I could distract him enough to prevent it, other times there was nothing I could do and would eventually succumb to it. But no matter how bad things got, I had some kind of awareness, even as early as seven-years-old, that he was more of a victim than I was. And I knew that the contorted spider-legged hands he used to crawl across my skin were just as useless to defend himself as mine were to me. At least that's what I believed.

Joseph, a Russian immigrant lived next door to Ben and his grandmother. An older man in his mid sixties, he stood tall and bore a strong militant presence. When Ben wasn't playing with me, he could usually be found shadowing Joseph, watching him work on things in his garage or following him into the bulkhead of his basement.

There was always something about Joseph that made me uneasy and told me to keep my distance. He confronted me once when someone had put a bumper sticker on his front door that read *"Russia Sucks."* I denied knowing anything about it even though I had heard a boy at school, Desmond, bragging about it. Joseph could tell I was hiding something, and the energy around him terrified me as he questioned everything I said.

While Ben had his moments of intimidating darkness, Joseph was always dark. Something in my gut always told me that Joseph had been the one to teach Ben the spider game.

Believing that Ben was also being molested left me with sympathy for him that somehow helped me to cope with what he was doing to me. I felt as though my suffering helped to ease his pain, and despite the devastating effects it had on me, I never held it against him or hated him for it. I accepted that part of him in the same way I accepted that he was hard of hearing and mentally disabled.

I learned to see the attacks coming on by tuning in to his expressions and mannerisms. I prepared myself a little better each time. I distracted myself by using my imagination and daydreaming about what I would be when I grew up. I had visions of someday being a rock star or a famous actor, and people would like me. I would have friends, and my family would be proud. Though my efforts to distract myself didn't always work, it sometimes helped me to push away the reality of what was happening at the moment. But inevitably it always caught back up with me, and I became more and more withdrawn.

Since Ben's spider game had become such a common event with us, he became more comfortable with it. It wasn't long before he was trying it on other kids in the neighborhood. But they were strong and confident and knew how to stop him, sometimes throwing punches and hitting him with rocks. Ben learned his lesson quickly as the younger neighborhood crowd began taunting him even more. He was given the nickname Spider Man and became notorious with the kids even outside our neighborhood. It killed me to see them gang up on him and tear him apart the way they did.

One day the Groton brothers pulled long, flexible branches from a forsythia bush and whipped him while he covered his eyes like a toddler trying to hide. He called out for his grandmother in a low drone that emphasized his hearing disability as the whips snapped against his body. The sound of him yelling out like that was heard often throughout the neighborhood, and it always made me nauseous and sad.

I would try to make them stop, but that made them focus on me too. Before long, word spread that I was sticking up for Spider Man and spending all my time with him. Though no one ever witnessed the molestation, they didn't have to. At that age, rumors carry more weight than any eyewitness account ever could. And just by my standing up for him, the rumors started. They spread like a brush fire across my neighborhood and through my school.

The onslaught that ensued was relentless. No one ever

spoke about it as child molestation or that it was wrong or that I should tell someone. No one ever showed sympathy or a willingness to help. And they certainly never showed mercy. Instead I was ridiculed by both the girls and the boys on a daily basis. "Don't stand next to him! He pulls his pants down." I was being called a faggot in the second grade and got spit at on a regular basis.

It was for that reason that I woke every morning with a burning, aching pain in the pit of my stomach. I constantly begged my mother to let me stay home from school.

"Mom, my stomach," I would groan while lying in bed, balled up in a fetal position.

She would walk in busily while getting ready for work and put her hand on my forehead. "You don't have a fever. You're going to school."

"Mom, please?"

"Craig, we are not going through this again. Nobody likes to get up in the morning. You're not sick. You're going to school. Get up!"

I literally begged her to let me stay home, sometimes crying uncontrollably on the floor. My excuse was always a stomach ache, the twisted, knotted-up, fiery pain of a stomach ache. But to her I was just a kid who didn't want to go to school. The truth was I really did have stomach aches. I was having anxiety and panic attacks at seven-years-old and living with a gut-wrenching fear on a daily basis. I often spent most of the day in the school nurse's office lying down across a row of chairs holding my belly and trying not to throw up at the thought of going back to class. I missed so much school, my mother finally brought me to a doctor.

"We better not be doing this for nothing," she said as we sat in bumper-to-bumper traffic with miles of street lights in front of us. We had little money at that time, and my pediatrician was deep in the inner city. "I had to take time out of work to do this."

I said nothing and stared down at my feet resting on the floorboards of the car. I pressed my hands against my stomach to make it hurt more. *If there isn't anything wrong with me, my mother is going kill me.*

The doctor took us in right away. His office was unlike a typical doctor's office. It was small and ran length-wise. It served as both a medical exam room and an actual office. At one end, a tall plant with big green leaves flopped heavily in all directions. Beside it was a dark wood desk covered in neatly stacked piles of manila folders. At the other end sat a standard faux leather examination table with a wide strip of white paper running across it. The walls were decorated with colorful graphics of the human body, and in the ceiling were two florescent lights, one at each end of the room.

My mother came in with me to discuss the situation with the doctor. He was a friendly looking white-haired man who was clearly approaching retirement. He had a gentleness about him that made him seem like the perfect grandfather, yet there was wisdom in his eyes that let you know he had truly seen it all.

"He says he has a stomach ache. He's always trying to stay home from school," my mother said.

"*Mmhhhmm*," the doctor mumbled as if ignoring my mother's claims until he determined his own diagnosis.

"What does it feel like, Craig?" he asked.

"It hurts," I said, holding my hands over my stomach.

"I need you to lie down for me, okay?"

I lay down on the table. The white paper crinkled under me as I carefully spun around, pulling my legs up with an exaggerated wince trying to prove to my mother that she didn't drive us down there for nothing.

"Does it hurt here?" he asked, pressing on the side of my ribs.

"It hurts everywhere." I whined.

"Craig, that's not even your belly," my mother jumped in. I instantly got nervous, fearing I had just confirmed her assumptions that nothing was wrong with me.

The doctor looked at me inquisitively as if he were hearing something I didn't say. He turned to my mother. "Would you mind waiting outside? I'd like to do a full physical examination on him," he asked my mother. She left the room to wait outside.

"Craig, I'd like to check everything out and make sure you're okay. Could you take off all your clothes except for your underwear?"

I did as he asked and sat back up on the table.

He paced and held his chin as if he had a suspicion to investigate. I sat on the edge of the table with my feet dangling over the edge. I was nervous that he wouldn't find anything and kept trying to focus on the knot in my stomach, hoping it would jump out at him. *See? I am sick. Tell my mom I don't have to go to school anymore.*

He switched off the light above the exam table. The room became dim with just the light at the other end on. It reminded me of my bedroom right before bedtime, when I kept a small lamp on as I got ready to sleep. "Do you play baseball, Craig?" he asked.

"No, I don't play any sports."

"You don't play sports?" His voice was exaggerated with surprise. "Why not?"

"I don't have anyone to play with."

He took one of my arms with one hand and placed the other hand on my shoulder. He slowly moved it in a circular motion massaging the joint. "Just relax," he said in a calming voice. "What about at school? You must play sports at school, no?"

"No." I looked at the floor, embarrassed that I didn't play anything.

He reached for my other arm, gently massaging my shoulder and then followed up with my wrists, knees, and ankles.

"I need you to lie back down on the table for me, okay?" I lay back on the table with my hands over my stomach to remind him I was too sick to go to school.

"So you don't have any friends, huh?"

"Not really," I said, thinking of Ben but too afraid to mention it. He was asking a lot of questions, and I didn't want him to go down that road.

"Just relax," he said again in a soft voice. He took my hands off my belly and laid my arms down at my side. I felt vulnerable lying there in only my underwear and my hands in a defenseless position. He put an open hand on my bare chest as if he were feeling my heartbeat and moved it around slowly feeling for the best spot to get the pulse. His other hand lay open on my belly slowly sliding across my skin and pressing down every so often.

My palms began to sweat and I twitched nervously. The feeling of hands on my skin was something I knew all too well. "Are you okay?" he asked, obviously sensing me getting uncomfortable.

"Yeah,Yeah. I-I'm Okay," I nodded.

He slid his hand down beneath the elastic band on my underwear pressing on my lower abdomen. I flinched and closed my eyes tight, bracing myself. My breath stopped for a moment, my body responded, waiting for what was coming next. He paused, pulled his hand back and took a deep breath letting out a powerful sigh. He turned away and ran his fingers through his white hair as if he had just discovered some terrible news he was hoping he wouldn't find.

"You can put your clothes back on, buddy. I'm going to talk with your mother for a minute." He went out in the hallway and closed the door behind him. I could hear voices discussing something that sounded important. I was nervous that he was telling my mother there was nothing wrong with me. Their voices continued, muffled, and indiscernible, but the tone escalated. After what seemed like an eternity they came back in the room. My mother had a stern expression about her. "Come on. Let's go." She reached for my hand and pulled me down the hallway.

"Mom, am I sick? What did he say?"

"You're fine. We'll come back another time."

The car ride home was quiet. My mother stared forward as if she were there alone. I was scared he had said there was nothing wrong with me, and I was now in trouble, or, worse, my stomach ache excuse wouldn't work anymore and I would have to go to school every day.

"Do I have to keep going to school?"

"Yes, Craig, you have to keep going to school. Everybody does."

I never found out what the doctor said to her, and we never went back to him again. The knot that made its home in my stomach continued to tangle, and the torture of elementary school never let up. The teachers rode me for my poor grades, and rumors continued to grow about me and Spider Man. I became more afraid of school than anything else at that time- even Ben. The unknown fear of what would happen each day was unbearable.

And on that particular afternoon, as I staggered home with blood dripping from my nose in the dead of winter, I had justification why.

Earlier that morning I had been at recess leaning against the brick wall of the school. A small inlet served as a hiding place where I spent most of my time to avoid being noticed by the other kids. It gave me a chance to be alone and feel safe for a few minutes a day. I loved hiding in there and watching the clouds pass by the ridgeline of the school's rooftop. If I squinted my eyes, it seemed as though the clouds were still and the school, instead, was moving. I had a fascination with that sight and spent every day pressing my back against the school and looking up, pretending that God held the clouds still for me while I pushed on the school and spun the whole earth. It was those kinds of moments that helped me to disconnect from what was all around me.

Unexpectedly, four girls approached from across the school yard and interrupted my imagination. They looked like they were on a mission. These weren't just any girls, either. These were the popular, pretty girls--the ones who were the envy of every other girl in school and the ones the boys were afraid to talk to. They set the trends and determined what was cool. Melinda was their leader and definitely the prettiest girl in our whole elementary school. She had amazing blue eyes that contrasted perfectly with her dark hair. The Correll twins were next in line. They were adored by most and virtually impossible to tell apart. Their mother dressed them the same every day and made sure their hair was always in perfect, elaborate styles with ribbons and bows. Then there was Jessica, another pretty girl who lived just a block away from the school. She was the quietest of the four, but when she spoke, she was mean.

Just the sight of them coming towards me made my stomach twist. *Please, God, don't let them talk about it. Don't let them say anything about it today.*

They confronted me in a semicircle, confident, like they

had just been given a dare and were proving they weren't scared to do it. "Is it true you pull your pants down?" Melinda asked with pure disgust.

"No," I said shyly, looking at the ground.

"I heard you get naked with some guy," one of the Correll twins said. The others squinted like they had just smelled something horrible.

"I don't. It's not true."

"Are you gay?"

"No."

"Why are you so gross?" Jessica asked, wrinkling her nose. "Do you even shower? Do you shower with men?"

They laughed and sneered like they had just scored a goal against an opposing team. *Please, God, make them go away.* My stomach twisted tighter. I looked at the ground. I wished I could blink my eyes and be home. I felt my back against the brick wall of the school and imagined I could push the world so fast it would make them fall over.

"You make the whole school stink. Do you know you smell that bad?"

I looked down at myself. I knew I didn't smell but my clothes were filthy. My mother had me doing my own laundry since I was old enough to drag a chair over to the machine and reach the buttons. But doing laundry is not a responsibility that a young boy takes seriously. I had scuff marks on my pants, my shirt was wrinkled, and my jacket was worn and dirty around the cuffs. I was a far cry from the Correll twins with the matching hairdos and ribbons that their mom did for them each morning. I wanted to cry, but instead tried with everything I could to hold back my tears. I hated them, I hated Ben, and I hated myself for being weak.

The circle around me had caught the attention of a few of the boys who were now coming over. I cowered backwards, pressing harder against the wall, and felt like I was going to throw up.

"Did you know Craig's gay?" Melinda asked Desmond, the boy who had put the "Russia Sucks" bumper sticker on Joseph's front door.

"Yeah and he smells like shit," Desmond responded as he stepped up to my face. "You smell like dog shit, faggot!"

My arms wrapped over my stomach to protect myself from a surprise uppercut to the belly. It had happened so many times in the past that I automatically covered my belly any time one of the boys came close to me.

"I'm going to kick your ass after school," he said.

The bell rang to go inside. Everyone scattered to get in line to go back in. For the rest of the day nearly everyone I passed made it a point to tell me that Desmond was going beat me up after school. Word spread about a fight and excitement grew with the passing minutes. There were few school buses. Most of the kids walked to school. Desmond and I took the same route home along with about a dozen other kids. Students who didn't even live in that direction talked about following us home just to watch Desmond pummel me.

At lunch I was too sick to eat, but that was usually the case anyhow. Eating was a humiliating experience for me by itself. Only a few kids in our school came from low-income families and qualified for free lunch, and I was one of them. The prepacked lunches came in small blue Styrofoam trays wrapped in cellophane and consisted of a soggy sandwich and a cookie. The blue tray was a dead giveaway that I was poor, and it was another thing for everyone to use against me.

Our school gymnasium doubled as the cafeteria, and

each morning the janitors wheeled out long rows of tables with benches on either side. The tables were assigned to us according to grade. I always sat alone at the end of the third-grade table. I preferred it that way. I never wanted anyone to sit next to me because I knew it would lead to something bad. If I could have eaten alone in a closet, I would have. I glanced down at the other end of the table to see the rest of the class chatting away. Several of them were making gestures to me with their fists as a reminder of what awaited me at the end of the day.

The rest of the afternoon, all I could think about was the fight. My stomach ached with a hot pain, and my eyes burned with restrained tears. I didn't know how to fight, and I didn't want to fight.

My older brother Jay had tried to teach me a few times, but it was no use. He was a tough kid who got into fights often. But I was nothing like him. He had no problem taking a punch and certainly had no problem delivering one. But I knew how bad it hurt to get hit. How could I ever make someone else feel that kind of pain? I was too afraid to punch people.

I knew I was going to get hurt because Desmond had beaten me up in the past. So I did the only thing I knew how to do to prepare for it: I prayed. I begged God to slow down the clock or make some miraculous chain of events occur that would get me home safely. I visualized Desmond somehow having a change of heart and coming over to apologize to me and tell me he was going to leave me alone.

At the end of the day I got ready to leave as fast as I could. I got my backpack and stood at the front of the line. I hoped if I had a head start, they wouldn't be able to catch me. I was the first one out the door and walked as fast as I could, but was careful not to move too fast. Maybe there was a slim chance that everyone had forgotten Desmond was going to beat me up. If I ran they might remember that I was a wanted man. I turned the corner at the end of the school yard to head down the street. My hurried pace made little difference and the crowd of more than a dozen kids was all but nipping at my heels in no time. Desmond came from behind and pushed me between my shoulder blades with both hands. My neck snapped back and I fell face-first into a puddle of ice water and slush. The heavy backpack strapped to my shoulders came down on me like a bag of bricks, knocking the wind out of me, and slid up over my head. My palms stung as they slapped against the cold wet pavement while I tried to break my fall. Everyone yelled out in excitement.

The stress of the day and the slam to the ground finally caught up with me and I burst into tears. I still didn't want to fight. I just wanted to go home. I just wanted to hide.

"Leave me alone!" I tried to stand up, but Desmond grabbed me in a headlock. His grip cut off my breathing, I tried everything to pull my head out, but he was too strong.

The crowd circled around us. "Punch him in the face!" "Hit him!" "Faggot!"

I tried to push him off while pulling my head out, but my ears peeled forward and stretched like they were tearing off.

Just as I felt myself about to black out, Desmond loosened his grip just enough to wind up his right arm and deliver an uppercut to my nose. I screamed. My head vibrated in pain and blood burst from my face. He hit me again and again, but his loosened grip was enough for me to slip my head out and cover my face with my raw, stinging palms.

The crowd quieted in disbelief. Blood dripped onto the ground in bright crimson splashes against the white mounds of snow. The kids who were yelling just a moment ago for him to hit me now stood shocked at the gory scene. I held my face and cried uncontrollably. Desmond backed up and looked surprised at the damage he had caused. Most of the crowd ran off as if my cries were an alarm system that had been set off across the entire city. The kids who stayed argued about who told Desmond to hit me, as if they feared getting into trouble as an accomplice.

I walked the rest of the way home from school with my head leaned forward to keep the blood from dripping on my clothes. I stumbled around like a drunken old man, sobbing uncontrollably as the winter air burned my lungs.

When I got to the front porch of our house I yelled for my mother. I was nearly hysterical, and I hated my life. I thought about my mom's temper, and Ben, how hard it was to never have my dad around, and school. I wished I was strong, I wish I was cool and people didn't pick on me. I wished I could fight. I was only in third grade and I hated everything about my life.

My mother came running to the door. "What the hell happened?" she asked with genuine concern.

"Desmond...beat...me...up," my words broke apart through my wails. I was having a nervous breakdown at seven-years-old right there on my front porch.

She lifted my head and looked at my bloody nose. "Calm down," she said, as if relieved that the only thing that happened was I got beat up. "Don't come in the house with that blood. Stay there."

I continued bawling. She came back with a wet kitchen towel and began wiping my face. I couldn't hold myself together.

"Okay, that's enough!" She was getting upset. "Relax. You're fine."

"I'm not fine. I don't want to go to school anymore. You don't understand!"

"Oh, come on! Stop it."

My body felt weak and exhausted, and my head vibrated in a pain so great, my teeth rattled.

"Listen." My mother stood up sharply, showing she had enough of the situation "That's enough. You can't come crying home to your mother every time you get hurt!"

She walked off in frustration to the kitchen sink, where she rinsed the blood from the towel while I stood alone and broken on the porch.

+++++

77

The memory began to dissolve into darkness like the others. I couldn't see anything, but I could hear and feel. My nose throbbed and burned with extraordinary pain from Desmond's punches. I tried to reach up to cover it, but my hands could not move.

A woman spoke anxiously. "Just keep pushing it in. It will go."

The throb in my nose turned to a sharp sting. I felt what seemed like a tube scraping against the soft flesh inside my nasal passage. I tried to move, to shake my head and turn away, but someone had their hands wrapped around it, holding me still. A teeth-gritting pain screamed through my entire head, and it felt like the tube was piercing the center of my brain and scraping its way down the back of my throat.

"Push it through. We need that in there now!" the woman's voice commanded.

I tried to scream but it only came as a low moan and my vocal cords tore with stinging shreds of pain. As quickly as I had regained this semi-conscious state, I again began to fall back out. The pain subsided and the voices faded away until another memory found its way into my vision.

6 THE HERO

I sat on the front steps of my mother's house and stared down at the end of the street, hoping the next car to turn the corner would be my dad's. He promised he was really coming this time, and I believed him, just as I always did. The anticipation taunted me while I pushed away the thought that maybe he wouldn't be coming. Maybe I would have to spend another week calling the bar, trying to get him to promise he would really come and get me the next time.

Ben paced the sidewalk in front of me picking at his eyebrows. "Kin you play, Craig?" he asked.

"No Ben, not today. My dad's coming to get me for a whole weekend," I answered proudly.

I was eight-years-old, and nearly six months had passed since I had seen my father. We talked often, though. I would call him nearly every night and leave messages at the bar for him. He was always happy to talk to me on the phone and always made plans to see me soon. "I'll be there right after school on Friday, how's that, pal?" he would say. I hardly slept waiting for him to come.

My mother would gently try to prep me for the inevitable. "Craig you know he might not come," she would say. But I wouldn't listen. At eight-years-old, I believed every word he said. My father was a super hero, and nothing could convince me otherwise. My mom would get so mad at him when he wouldn't show up week after week that she would start telling me about all the horrible things my dad used to do to her: how he choked her unconscious one time and how his anger was uncontrollable after the war. She would pull out pictures from their wedding and make me look at how drunk he was. Every time he blew off another weekend with me and I was left heartbroken, she would have to clean up the mess. It killed her that I didn't hate him like she did.

I pulled a pack of Marlboro Reds from my pocket and a lighter with the Miller beer logo on it that I got for my dad. I had saved up pennies and loose change from our couch cushions for the last couple months and bought them from Mrs. Stanley who owned the corner store at the end of our street. She worked the front counter, and her husband worked a small deli they had set up in the back. The Stanleys were good people and knew we had little money. They would let my mother buy food and cigarettes on credit and pay for them in installments.

Mrs. Stanley had been hesitant to sell me the cigarettes because, for one, I was paying with cash, and two, she knew my mother didn't smoke Marlboros. She obviously assumed they were for me and drilled me on the dangers of smoking.

"I swear they're for my dad. He's coming to get me this weekend." Getting my dad a present was easy for me. He was a very simple man and he liked only a few things. He was a Marine who served in Vietnam; he smoked Marlboros, drank Miller beer, had pictures of Jesus in his apartment, and listened to Elvis. That was pretty much it. Anything in one of those categories would make him happy.

I smiled at the lighter in my hand, thinking of how clever it was that I killed two birds with one stone: Marlboros and a Miller beer logo. Too bad the lighter wasn't in the shape of Elvis' head, I thought. The sight of another car rounding the corner caught my eye but I quickly knew it wasn't him. I had his car memorized: a 1980 Oldsmobile Cutlass. I knew its boxy shape, the silver-and-maroon two-tone paint job, the sputtering sound of the exhaust, everything. I could tell in a split second, as soon as I saw the first inch of a car rounding the corner if it was him or not. And when it wasn't, I was one car closer to seeing my dad.

I closed my eyes for a moment and thought, "Okay, I'm going to count to three. When I open my eyes, his car will be there. Ready? One, two, three." I opened my eyes with a pop, hoping to see him driving up the road and waving his arm out the window at me with a big smile. But no such luck.

I had been sitting on the steps for nearly an hour already. It only took about fifteen minutes to drive from his house to ours. He lived on the other side of the city, but the highway cut right through all the traffic and it was an easy drive. I ran back in the house to call the bar and see if he had left yet. I had to be quick in case he was pulling in the street while I was making the call.

"Eden's!" Carlo answered with a loud declaration. Carlo was the kind of guy with dreams of being in the mafia but couldn't quite make the cut. He drove a Lincoln, wore oversized gold rings, and left the top few buttons of his shirt wide open all the time. He was a good guy to me and gave me free Shirley Temples and Slim Jims when my dad brought me to the bar. I had known him since I could remember and every time I walked in he would say, "Bobby, is that your boy? Wow, you double in size every time I see you, kiddo."

"Is Bobby Miller there?" I asked hesitantly, hoping he would say "Nope, he already left to go pick you up."

Carlo knew my voice well. I called there for my dad all the time, plus I'm sure he didn't get many calls from eight-year-olds.

"Bobby, it's your boy," he yelled. I could hear him stretching the telephone cord across the bar.

"Yeah, pal, what's up?"

"Dad, I thought you were coming today?"

"Yeah, I am. Don't worry. I ah, I'll be there in about a half hour."

"Ok, Dad. Hurry!"

I ran back outside and onto the steps to take up my position scouting the end of the street. The only car that rounded the corner was Steve's. He and my mother were engaged now, and things were tense between me and him. I knew he was going to be with us for a while, and it never sat well with me. My mother wasn't home from work yet, and the tangled knot that lived in my stomach tightened with the thought of seeing him alone. Usually I would sit on the curb down on the other end of the street and wait until I had seen my mother's car before I went home.

Steve was a very different person when she was around. He was a lot nicer to me and hid a lot of his resentment toward me. But today I didn't care. My dad was on his way, and he was going to get me out of here for an entire weekend. Maybe we would play miniature golf or shoot empty beer bottles off the wall in his backyard with pellet guns. I didn't care, as long as I got to spend time with him.

Steve stepped out of his truck. Grease covered his dark blue Dicky pants and work shirt. He was a machinist. It was a stressful blue-collar job that "paid the bills" and "put food on the table." He worked for a big company, and I don't know where he sat on the totem pole, but by the way he often came home from work I would guess it was somewhere near the bottom. He had a lit cigarette clenched in his teeth and carried a huge black lunch box.

"What are you doing out here?" he snarled.

"My dad's coming to get me today!"

"Ha, no, he's not!" He smirked, walking past me into the house and flicking his cigarette on the ground in front of me.

About another half hour had gone by, and I knew my dad would be here any minute. I saw my mother round the corner, coming home from work. I could see a look of concern and frustration on her face as she pulled in the driveway. She stepped from her car quickly. "Craig, why don't you wait inside?"

"I don't want to. He's going to be here any minute."

"When did he tell you he was coming?" she asked with obvious disbelief.

"He said he was coming in a half hour and that was a half hour ago."

Her frustration quickly changed to anger with the slam of her car door. She knew he was supposed to pick me up right after school, and that was over two hours ago. She walked into the house. I could hear her throw her pocket book on the table with a splash of makeup cases and loose change. I stayed on the porch steps, watching the end of the street, and could hear her inside on the phone.

"Let me talk to Bobby Miller," she said. "Bobby, I am not going to spend another weekend cleaning up your mess. He has been out on the porch waiting for you now for over two hours." Her voice was stern and very serious. She paused briefly to listen to whatever it was he was saying.

"Don't bullshit me! I am not an eight-year-old boy who's going to believe your lies. If you don't come and get him now, you will never see him again. I'm not going to do this anymore." She slammed the phone down and came back outside.

"Craig, he's still at the bar. Why don't you come wait inside?" Her voice was sharp and riddled with her anger about the situation, but she did her best to sound sympathetic.

"I'll just stay here mom. It only takes a few minutes for him to get here." She shook her head in frustration and went back inside.

It was getting dark now and harder to see the colors of the cars, but about forty-five minutes later I saw it: The front passenger side of the maroon Oldsmobile swung a hard right and started up the street. I jumped from the steps and ran to the end of the driveway. "Mom, he's here!" I yelled back to the house.

My mother stood in the front door with a hard glare looking at my dad, who waved to her like nothing was wrong.

I threw my bag in the back and jumped into the front seat. "I got you presents, Dad!" I excitedly gave him the cigarettes and lighter I had in my pocket.

"Thanks buddy," he said, reaching over and scruffing up my hair--his usual welcoming hug. It was true. It was really true! I was spending an entire weekend with my dad!

When we got to the other side of the city, we pulled off the highway and made our way up Hilton Street or "the hill" as my dad always called it. He had lived in the area all his life, moving from one apartment to another but never leaving the vicinity of the hill. Even after he joined the Marines to fight in Vietnam, he went right back there. It was a tough area that stretched for about five or six blocks in all directions, mostly made up of three-deckers, shoddy city playgrounds, and run-down corner stores. In the middle of everything was a barroom called Eden's Inn. It was my dad's second home. When he was a kid he lived in the apartment above it. I once heard a story that his mom and dad had a fight, and she made his father sleep on the couch. His dad was so angry about it, he chopped the couch up with a machete and threw it out the window to the street. I never knew my dad's parents, they both died when he was still a teenager--but knowing my dad, I never doubted that story for a second.

As we made our way up the hill, I put my hands under my legs and crossed my fingers, hoping he wouldn't stop at the bar. I was happy to be with him, but nearly every time he took me for the weekend or even just for an afternoon we would stop there. Sometimes we would stay till closing and then return the next morning, spending eight or ten hours straight sitting on bar stools, watching a sports game, and listening to my dad and his buddies swap stories about divorce and child support.

I didn't mind it much. It actually made me feel cool: a young kid in a tough bar for the weekend. Imagine if the kids at school could see me now. I bet their dads never let them hang out in a barroom until two in the morning. The thought of feeling cool wore off quickly though, and after a while, it got real boring. Some of the guys would slide quarters down the bar to me so I could play the pinball machine in the corner, but that lasted only a short while. At times I slept in a chair while my dad drank twelve or eighteen beers deep into the night.

He pulled the car over to the side of the road just as I hoped he wouldn't, and I knew we were headed for another night at the bar. No big deal, I thought. We went in and the familiar smell of beer-stained carpet and stale cigarettes filled the air.

"Bobby, that your boy?" Carlo yelled from behind the bar.

"Yeah, you believe this? He's gotten so big, I bet he can kick your ass," my dad yelled out as he rubbed his hand on the top of my head.

"Hey, don't doubt it, Bobby," Carlo yelled back. "I'm sure he'll be kicking your ass soon, too."

We went over to the bar, and Carlo brought me a Coke before I could even shimmy up on the bar stool. "Hey, buddy," he said to me with a wink. "Why don't you show your old man he ain't as tough as he thinks he is?"

I smiled at the thought of myself being as tough as my dad.

I looked down the bar to see the regulars. Whitey, a white-haired old man who gave me dollar bills every time I saw him. Roley, his real name was Roland--he was a portly guy so the name Roley suited him well. Eddy, Smitty, and a few others were always there too, but I never really knew them.

We had been there a couple hours. The night got busy. It had been dark for a while now, and the bar was filled with weekend bar-hoppers along with all the regulars. It was loud and chaotic, everyone talking over each other. Arms brushed past me as people reached over the bar to pass drinks and money. Suddenly, through the commotion, I saw my brother Jay walking in through the door. My eyes went wide with surprise; it wasn't often that I saw him, and it was almost never when I was with my dad. My brothers and I had different fathers, but my dad adopted them while he was married to my mom. After the divorce, my brothers saw him even less than I did.

"Hey, buddy," Jay said with a big smile.

"Jay!"

He had a determined look about him like he was on a mission he was scared to accept but did it anyway. "Do you want to go the drive-in movies with me tonight?"

I looked at my dad with an excited smile as if I were asking permission to go but before I could speak my dad barked, "What the fuck are you doing?" at my brother.

"What?" Jay asked, although his obvious intention was to get an eight-year-old boy out of the bar in the middle of the night. "I just thought he'd want to see a movie or something."

In a lightning-quick reaction, my father grabbed Jay by his shirt with two fists and drove him backwards through the door and out onto the sidewalk. The bar-hoppers jumped up, alert, as if a brawl was about to start, while the regulars remained seated sipping their drinks. Through the window, I could see my dad slam my brother against the wall. The red neon glow of a beer sign lit up his face and accentuated the anger in his eyes.

"Are you calling me a bad fucking father?" he screamed an inch from Jay's face.

My brother was a tough kid and thought nothing of hitting anybody who got in his face, but my father's temper was legendary. They exchanged a few more words. Jay pushed my father's arms off him and came quickly walking back into the bar, determined to fulfill his mission. He put on the best smile he could, hoping I had not seen everything that had just happened. "Do you want to go to the drive-in with me or stay here with Dad?"

I felt torn but the fact was, seeing my dad was a pretty

rare thing. "I'll stay here with Dad."

"Okay, pal, if you change your mind, just call me."

My brother left, and we stayed at the bar until closing. But the rest of the night my dad was withdrawn. He drank his beer and looked off into the bottle-lined wall behind the bar. When Carlo closed up for the night we went back to my father's apartment. On the way I was beginning to doze off and leaned my head against the window of the car. "I'm not a bad father, am I?" my dad asked out of nowhere.

"No, Dad, you're the best," I said, surprised by the question.

"You love me, don't you?"

"Of course I love you."

He didn't say a word after that.

My father lived in a building with nine apartments. It was situated at the end of a torn-up road just off the hill in a tightly compacted neighborhood made up mostly of beat-up three-story houses and run-down cars. My dad knew just about everybody around there and was close with all the guys in his building. My uncle Bob lived right upstairs from my dad and my uncle Jim above that. The rest of the guys were part of the crowd they had grown up with. The entire building was made up of divorced Vietnam veterans who received a less-than-warm welcome when they returned from the war. Their story was summed up by a simple, hand-painted sign hanging over the entry way to the building that read, "The Castaways."

The building was a terrifying place, and it had a very unsettling feel to it, especially to an eight-year-old boy. Even more unsettling, my dad's apartment was part of the basement. It was small with exposed pipes in the ceiling and a cold concrete floor. I had to sleep on a love seat in the living room, and I hardly caught a wink when I was there. I constantly kept one eye open, concerned about things going bump in the night. The building was well-known to be haunted. About ten years before, a man was murdered in the apartment upstairs for not paying a debt. The killer broke in through the window, slaughtered the man's dog, and then murdered the man while he was in the shower. Everyone in the building shared stories of a dog barking in the next room or footsteps running up and down the stairs. Some even claimed to have been touched by something that wasn't there. My dad and his brothers would get drunk and leave out bowls of dog food, hoping to appease the ghost.

We got up the next morning and went to one of the city's filthy boxcar diners for breakfast, then headed back to Eden's for the rest of the day and well into the night. Lunch and dinner was made up of sour-cream potato chips, Slim Jims, and pickled eggs. My dad remained quiet and withdrawn. He didn't join in the usual barroom chatter with all the regulars and spoke very little to me.

Sunday morning he woke up even more detached, as if he had the world on his shoulders or was nursing a bad hangover. I knew a hangover was unlikely, since his blood pretty much ran with alcohol 24/7. He was a solid drinker, and most of time I couldn't even tell he was drunk.

I sat on the love seat and watched him getting ready for the day in his bedroom, which wasn't much bigger than most people's closets. He had a twin mattress pressed into the corner. His night stand was a cardboard sonotube with a piece of plywood on top. A black and white TV hung by chains from the ceiling above a bureau with a tall skinny mirror.

He put on a red T-shirt with the words *Semper Fi* across the front and the US Marine Corps logo on the back. I watched him standing in front of the mirror with a blank expression, as if he were trying to hide something from even himself. He ran a flat plastic comb through his hair, and I wondered for a moment what I would look like at his age. He gently put the comb down on the bureau and walked over to a shelf on his wall. He stood in front of a faded yellowed statue of the bust of Jesus. A crack that had once divided it in two shone with a bead of discolored glue. In the center of the bust was the bright red heart of Christ. My father reached out and put his finger on the heart and put his other hand on his own, like we did at school when we pledged allegiance to the flag. He bowed his head and stood silent.

"Let's go to church today, okay?" he said abruptly.

"Okay, Dad." I was never a big fan of church, but I was relieved we were taking a break from the bar.

"Does your mother take you to church?" he asked with a hardened expression.

"No."

He shook his head and mumbled something under his breath, clearly making his own judgment about her parenting skills.

Mass had already begun by the time we got there, but that was my dad's way. He always went in after it had started and left before it ended, but while he was there, he made the most of the opportunity and got right to the point.

We slowly opened a tall door in the back corridor of the church to an enormous room that looked like the inside of an alien fortress. Huge pillars stretched to the ceiling and arched outward in all directions with elaborately painted stonework. The walls were lined with stained glass windows that seemed to have the power to control the sunlight and transform it into colors and shapes that beamed into the room. A crowd of hundreds stood before us, holding books and reciting words in perfect unison. And in the middle of it all, up at the front hanging from the ceiling, was an immense statue of Christ on the cross. I thought of the painting in my room, and despite the overwhelming awe of the building I had just walked into, I felt like I had some connection with being there.

My father walked in front of me and entered a pew in the back, where he quietly knelt and bowed his head. I stood fixated on the incredible size and shape of the room and the huge crowd that filled the rows of wooden benches. It seemed that everyone knew what to do without being told. I felt like I was watching a well-rehearsed performance from the back of the stage. I watched as the crowd knelt, stood, sat, read from books, and sang in perfect harmony, all while my father remained on his knees with his head down and eyes closed. He ignored the entire performance as if he were the only one in the room.

The priest spoke from the front with a voice that reverberated through even the tiniest of spaces in the intricate stone work. The crowd sat quietly, and listened as if they were being given important instructions. I tried to understand him, but his words were hard to follow and his voice seemed to overlap itself in the echoes around me. But I listened nonetheless, and I watched, entranced by the conviction of his voice and the power he held over the room.

"And in these words we are shown the grace of our Lord God," he said. "For God so loved the world, that He gave His only begotten Son, that whoever believes in Him shall not perish, but have eternal life."

My father unfolded his hands and lifted his head as if he no longer needed to be there.

"Dad," I whispered. "What does that mean?"

He slid himself across the pew and took my hand, leading me out the same way we came in. "It means if you believe in God, then He'll believe in you. Let's go." His voice was distant and detached, but his words made sense to me and penetrated the mesmerizing trance I was in.

We got outside and the solemn look he had worn on his face for the last two days seemed even more amplified. "What's the matter, Dad?"

"Nothing, pal, I'm okay. Let's get something to eat."

We drove to a city diner and he parked the car on the side of the street beneath a highway overpass. The morning was gray, and the color of the carbon-stained cement and iron highway construction beams blended into the sky. Beside us was an abandoned railway terminal where my dad used to work before he got laid off years before. Newspapers and city trash blew across the streets and shuffled in the air with the passing cars.

He pulled the keys from the ignition but made no attempt to get out of the car. He took a deep breath, laid his hands on the steering wheel, and stared straight ahead.

"Dad, are you okay?" I began getting nervous. My father was never like this. Something was wrong.

"Dad?"

He continued staring ahead, his hands still on the wheel with a white-knuckle grip. "Daddy, what's wrong?"

He exhaled slowly, and a tear dripped from his eye and down his cheek. I unbuckled my seatbelt and jumped up, kneeling on the seat to face him. I had never seen him so distraught, and I had never seen him cry. He was a superhero soldier. He was strong and tough. My heart raced in confusion and panic. "Dad! Dad, what's wrong? Daddy?" I moved across the front seat on my knees and reached up, putting my arms around his neck.

"Daddy, don't cry! Please. Everything's okay." My words cracked at the sight of my father crying, and tears puddled in my eyes while I watched him begin to crumble. I was never so scared and confused. He let go of the wheel and turned to hug me back. He held me tighter than he ever had before. It was a real hug. It wasn't a hand reaching out to scruff up my hair, and it wasn't a pat on the back. It was a real hug from my father. I felt him shake as he fought to keep his tears in and himself together. His breath was slow and steady. He loosened his arms and pulled back just far enough to put his head down in front of mine, and he reached up to wipe his eyes.

"Daddy, what's wrong?"

He covered his face with both his hands and wiped away his tears, to gain back his composure. He took a deep breath, lifted his head, and looked at me with the eyes of a person I had never met before.

"I've done some terrible things in my life."

I pulled him back in, hugging him as hard as I could. "It's okay, Daddy. You're not going to get in any trouble. Everything's okay," I said, trying to understand the extent of what he meant.

"I'm so sorry," He whispered under his breath, as if he were speaking to a world that would never hear him.

+++++

I held my father in my arms and saw the gray city that surrounded us slowly fading to black. I tightened my grip trying to keep the memory with me, but there was nothing I could do. He slowly dissolved in my arms, and I was left alone in complete darkness.

"Craig?" I heard my father's voice. It sounded as fragile and vulnerable as it had that morning in the car. "Craig, wake up, pal. Come on," he whispered.

I struggled to understand what was happening. The vision of that morning was so vivid, yet I knew I wasn't there anymore. Yet I could still hear him speaking with the same familiar frailty of that day.

"Come on, pal. Wake up, Craig, please." He spoke so softly.

I heard the desperation in his words and the burden in his heart. I heard him exhale a long deep breath of exhaustion. And in my confusion, in my search to understand where I was and what was happening, I felt the warm sensation of his hands taking mine. I felt them shake with a nervous strength, and I felt his skin in amazing detail with every scrape and every scar.

As I lay balanced on the edge of death in my own private darkness, I felt the hands of my father. I felt the determination in them that worked tirelessly to make a living. I felt the love in them that once held my mother and placed a ring on her finger in commitment. I felt the fear in them that desperately clenched the barrel of a gun and bravely but hesitantly pulled a trigger for his country. I felt the remorse that pressed them together in the back of a city church every Sunday. And I felt the hands that scruffed my hair when I was a boy and patted me on the back. I heard his voice, and I felt his hands, the hands of my father.

I lay in the darkness, a seemingly lifeless body, feeling his touch. And in that moment I saw the significance of the memory I had just relived. I saw the vivid setting of the gray city. I felt the confusion and concern that made me want to hold him as he cried. And I saw the morning when my father, the most hardened man I knew, showed me his heart and taught me a lesson in humility.

I wanted so badly to wake up. I wanted to jump up and tell him I was okay and that I heard him and felt him. I wanted to reach out and hold him like I had that morning when I was eight years old. But I couldn't move. I couldn't even speak, and the thought of falling back into unconsciousness turned my stomach. I felt the sensation of his hands slowly begin to fade as I went numb and began to slip away.

7 THE SIGN

My father had built a barroom in the basement of my mother's house before their divorce. Complete with faux leather couches, a fully stocked bar with matching bar stools, a TV hung from chains, and glowing beer signs all around the room. Above the bar was a red and gold sign that read "Miller's Cave." It was a fairly impressive set up. There was no food in the house and the electricity was shut off half the time, but we had a pretty nice barroom in our basement. I was so young when he and my mom divorced, I don't remember him building it. I just knew of it always being there, and to me that basement barroom became a way to imagine my dad still living at home. When he wouldn't show up to get me for weekend visits, I would go down downstairs and imagine he was with me. I would put stuffed animals on the barstools and pretend to be a bartender serving up the regulars. It was a strange getaway for a young boy, but it meant everything to me. It was the only thing I had to make me feel like I was with my dad, and I found comfort in knowing he had made everything down there, even the red and gold "Miller's Cave" sign.

I was still in elementary school when Steve and my mother got married. He had been living with us only a short while when they decided to make the commitment. This wasn't anything unusual. My mother fell in love pretty easily and this was her fourth marriage.

The ceremony was in a Justice of the Peace's basement. Only a few close friends and family were invited, but it was a big crowd for such a tight space. Everyone lined up on either side of a pool table in the center of the room while my mother and Steve were at the end of the table with the JP. There wasn't a big reception or a honeymoon. They both had been married previously and chose to forgo the traditional procedure. A lack of money to even pay the bills made that decision easier for them.

I sat in the back of my new stepfather's station wagon for the ride home after the ceremony. The words *Just*

Married covered the back window and empty beer cans and streamers dragged behind us. I leaned my head against the window and couldn't help but wonder what it was like when Mom and Dad got married. I wished I had seen them that day when they were happy together and actually talked to each other. It killed me to think they weren't in love and a stepfather was living in our house instead of my real dad. And Steve's strong presence did not help the situation.

My mom was a single woman who took care of three boys with only a fast-food cashier's paycheck. She sought her knight in shining armor, and in her eyes, Steve was that knight. Unfortunately, he knew it. He knew she needed him, and he knew he was there to straighten things out and to "rescue" her. He moved right in with a "new sheriff in town" attitude and had no problem taking over our home. He would joke and say things like, "I'm the king of this castle now." In reality, he wasn't joking. His philosophy was, "I pay the bills; this is my house now." He often followed up with, "as long you live under my roof, you will live by my rules."

Those lines crippled me, and he and my mother both said them often. The two of them might as well have been saying "We are not a family, this is not a home, and you are only living here because I let you," which wasn't far from the truth. My mother made it clear right from an early age that when my brothers and I turned sixteen, we had to start paying rent. This wasn't designed to teach a lesson in responsibility; it was a well-planned strategy to get us out of the house. It was common knowledge that when we were eighteen we had to leave. She would openly talk to friends and family mimicking what she would say when we turned eighteen: "That's it, you're out! My job is over. I'm done taking care of you. Get out." Steve supported her in this, and they fed off each other.

Though they shared similar values in their outlook on children, one major difference stood out in their union. Since I was my mother's last child and so much younger than my brothers, she considered me her "baby." It was no secret that I didn't like Steve, and my mother let my voice be heard at times. "You don't have to love him, but you do have to respect him," she would say. But I found it very difficult to respect a man who didn't respect me. It became an issue between them. They often fought about the tension between me and Steve, and my mother did her best to help us get along.

One night I got up to get a glass of water and found them both drunk, sitting on the kitchen floor. The lights were low, and a Patsy Kline record played in the background. The room felt thick with tension and uneasy emotion. My mother sat leaning against the stove crying while Steve sat quiet at the opposite side of the room.

She pulled me into her lap and held me in a drunken hug. "I want you to tell Steven you love him," she slurred. "Go tell him please, for me?" Despite my reluctance, I did it, assuming any lack of cooperation would have some serious repercussions.

Their conflict over my place in the house grew stronger once my brothers left. Steve had a big issue with Jay and gave my mother an ultimatum: "either he leaves, or I leave." My mother chose her husband and kicked Jay out of the house. He was sixteen years old.

The decision happened in a split second one night. My mother and Steve were already in the midst of a drunken argument when Jay came home with a new motorcycle. My mother forbade him from keeping the bike, but Jay refused to return it. Steve went outside and tried ripping all the wires and hoses off of it so it couldn't be driven. When Jay stepped in to stop him, fists started flying. I watched the whole thing unravel outside my bedroom window as my brother and step-father rolled across our lawn, throwing punches at one another. My mother screamed in hysterics while my brother, Tyler, tried to break it up.

When the fistfight was over, Jay left, but the chaos continued. Tyler stayed in my room with me while my mother and Steve tore the entire house apart.

The next day, when Jay got home from school, my mother had a note waiting for him on the kitchen table. He was to leave immediately.

To see him pack his things solidified for me how weak our family was. He went to live with one of his friends' parents on the other side of the city and I never saw much of him from then on.

Not long after, my brother Tyler left, too. He made the decision to go on his own before he became a target. But I was much too young to go be going anywhere soon. With my brothers out of the way, Steve turned his attention to me.

He was sly in his tactics. He avoided any outright torment while my mother was around. He saved his best for when we were alone, which was nearly every day. He got home from work about two hours before my mother did. Things got so bad for a while that I preferred to stay down the street at Ben's house. Steve's big thing was making sure I kept my room clean. When I got home from school and it was just him and me, he would tell me to clean my room and then have "inspections," pointing out lint in the carpet or dust on the furniture.

One day Steve decided I had failed his inspection too many times. He stood in the doorway while I crawled across the floor of my bedroom. For almost an hour, he had been pointing out imperfections in my cleaning habits. With the sternness of a drill sergeant, he yelled out insults and commands. "You call this fucking clean? What the fuck is this?" His finger shook and veins popped in his forearm as he pointed to anything that did not satisfy him. "Clean this fucking room!"

My tears dripped onto the floor. I crawled from one spot to another and used my fingernails to pick the tiniest of things from the carpet. The twisted pain in my stomach that had been with me for years had become a living, breathing beast. And at moments like this, it felt like a wild dog clawing at me from the inside.

"You fucking cry baby! How old are you, ten? You're a ten-year-old little fucking baby. You want to cry like a baby? You know what babies do? Get the fuck up!" He pulled me up by my shoulders and effortlessly threw me onto the armchair in the living room. "You want to be a fucking baby? Here then, baby, watch cartoons, you little crying shit." He yelled and mocked me by rubbing his eyes as if he were crying like an infant. He set the TV to a cartoon channel and turned back to me. "Watch cartoons like babies do you, little shit."

About an hour later my mother arrived home. Steve was calmly sitting on the couch, and I was still in the chair where he had thrown me. It was obvious to her that I had been crying.

"What happened?" she asked.

Steve's tone was nonchalant.

"I don't know," he said. "He didn't want to clean his room and got all upset when I asked him to." My mother did nothing and only gave me another lecture about how I didn't have to love him, but I did have to respect him.

A couple days later I sat on the front porch steps waiting for my dad to pick me up. He was supposed to be there Friday after school, but that had changed to Saturday morning. Now it was half past four and becoming obvious that this was going to be another weekend without my dad. I was peering off down at the bottom of the street waiting for his car to take the corner when my stepfather came out to the porch.

"Give this to your father," he said with a smirk and

dropped a piece of wood in my lap. It was the red and gold sign that read "Miller's Cave."

My dad never showed up that night, and Sunday didn't happen, either. I went to the basement like I always did when I missed him, and hanging above the bar was a brand new red and gold sign that read "Tackett's Tavern"- my mother's new last name.

I needed out. I was overcome with determination that welled within me. This was not my family, this was not my house, and this was not how I wanted to live my life. I stood in the basement of my mother's house looking up at that sign and, at ten years old, I knew that I did not belong there anymore

+++++

The vision of the basement turned to black, and that feeling of determination settled in my core. I had to make a change in my life. I had to get out. I had to move.

My body pulsed in a reflexive reaction to the thoughts I had from that memory. I felt my heart expanding and my blood flowing beneath my skin. I felt an awareness of the darkness. I can't stay here anymore. I've had enough.

"Craig, you need to calm down. You're in the hospital,

honey. We're trying to help you," an unfamiliar woman's voice said, barely making its way into my comprehension. "Just try to relax."

Then without warning I was out again.

8 THE MOVE

I put the last of my things in a box labeled *Craig's Room*. It was moving day, and we were leaving. I had longed to get out of that house ever since that day in the basement. I prayed every morning and every night to God. It was a routine I never swayed from. "Please take me out of here. Please move us far away, away from Ben, away from my school, and away from my whole life. Please don't let anyone know where we are going and don't let them follow me. I promise that I won't tell anyone that it was you who made it all happen. It will be our secret."

Although life carried on as usual and the light never appeared at the end of the tunnel, I always had a deep belief that my prayers would be answered. And here it was: moving day.

The circumstances weren't entirely perfect. Steve's father was moving out of his house and had offered to sell it to him and my mother at an exceptionally low price. Given that it was Steve's house and that he still had his "king of the castle" attitude, I knew I would be a peasant living in his kingdom. But none of that mattered. I was a teenager leaving all fourteen years of my life behind me and moving more than twenty miles outside the city. I had the opportunity to start a new life with new faces and maybe even new friends. The kids I grew up with wouldn't be able to ridicule me anymore, and Ben would never be able to touch me again.

The house was nearly empty. The curtains were packed away, and the summer sun shone freely through my bedroom window. I had never felt the house so light and open. It was a strange experience to look around and see everything gone. It was almost like the slate was wiped clean, and it made me feel as light as the house looked.

I reached up and pulled the last thing that I had to pack off my wall: the black velvet painting of Christ. A clean, rectangle shape still remained on the wall surrounded by years of fading wallpaper.

I held the canvas in my hands and thought of the times when I was younger, when I had spent so many nights cowering in fear while I stared into the bursting sun on the painting and begged God to hear me. I remembered how I wrote the note to Him just a few days before Christmas and how I was overwhelmed with the need to write a message never to forget how I felt. And I thought of all the times I ran my fingers over the crimson color that dripped from the cross, begging for God to be with me and believing that he somehow was.

I had prayed for years for things to change, for us to move away, for anything different. I made compromises: "If you make this go away, I promise I'll pray every day. I'll do anything you want. Just tell me and I'll do it. I swear." I begged and I pleaded, but above all I believed. And it happened. It came true. We were moving. From circumstances without any hope for change came an unexpected chain of events that played out perfectly, and my prayers were answered. God was more real to me than He had ever been and I felt the truth of the words my father had said to me in the back of a city church on a dreary Sunday morning: If I believe in God, then He would believe in me.

I placed the painting on top of the box and walked through the house for the last time. The living room was empty and the missing furniture left islands in the carpet where years of heavy footsteps had worn pathways around them. The wallpaper, shaded in a yellow smoke-stained hue, highlighted the scrapes and dents from years of violent outbursts. I pushed the bathroom door open with the box that I held in my arms and took one last look in a cracked mirror. *Tomorrow I was going to be a whole new person in a new town with a brand-new life. Tomorrow I will have left the memories of this house behind.*

I made my way out to the truck where my mother and Steve were loading the last of their things. We drove off down the street and I watched the house fade from sight. The school year was over, and I never told anyone that we were moving. I never mentioned it to my teachers or any of the kids. And I never told Ben that I was going away and not coming back. I closed my eyes, thanked God for listening and felt something I had never experienced before in my life: optimism. When we arrived at the new house, I couldn't help but be taken aback by the name of our new street: Faith Avenue.

The new neighborhood was different than what I was used to. It had brightness and a sense of freedom in the air. Houses lined the street like rows of garden flowers. Deep green lawns served as giant welcome mats with flat, even surfaces and perfectly straight lines, trimmed to the finest detail. A swimming pool next door sparkled a crystalline blue as if it were reflecting a cloudless sky. Faces were friendly and words were kind.

But the move brought more than just a change of scenery; it brought a change of just about everything. It gave my mother the opportunity to get a new job working in an office. She made enough money to furnish our new house. That ability gave her a sense of pride that she never had before. The violent outbursts that ruined our old house became a thing of the past. She still drank just as often and kept true to the unpredictable mood swings she was known for, but nothing got broken.

For my stepfather the new house was all about pride, too. He became obsessed with remodeling and constantly looked for things to rebuild or redesign.

"You have the whole summer off," he said to me as we stared out into the thick woods that bordered the edge of our backyard. "You're not going to sit around and do nothing. I want you to get all of these bushes out of here." He pointed to a spread of dense thornbushes that grew out of control and blanketed the woods at the edge of our yard. "We're going to build a fireplace here, and I don't want to look out at all of this shit. I want it gone by the end of the summer, are we clear? Tear them up by the roots so they don't come back."

His attitude was just as I had expected. He came home every day and inspected the work he had left for me to do. Nothing was ever good enough, and he officially nicknamed me "Half-Ass" because, as he put it, everything I did was done half-ass. To be honest, I never put much effort into anything Steve wanted me to do for him. I had no more desire to make him happy than he did to make me happy. And none of his comments mattered to me anymore. Dealing with him became easier than it had ever been. This was a new life for me. I wasn't about to spend my summer cleaning up his yard and taking care of his house. This summer was my first chance to be left alone without having so much to worry about. And I did everything I could to use my time for just that. I was ready to leave my old life behind.

I spent every day in my room alone, isolated from the world. I preferred the solitude, despite the welcoming feel of the neighborhood outside my window. It was the first time in my life that I had a chance to breathe, to let down my guard and try to reset myself. I did nothing but listen to music, all day every day. The songs filled my need for companionship.

I made it my mission to decipher the words to every song I heard. It fascinated me to see that someone could write such amazing poetic verses about how they felt. I lined the walls of my room with open CD jackets so I could see the lyrics. I listened to songs on the radio over and over, and wrote down everything I heard in stacks of notebooks. I read them back, line by line, and sought out the true meaning of each song. I loved it: the process, the songs, the words, the culmination of melody and poetry, and the depth of each verse. I spent the entire summer locked away in my room listening, reading, thinking, and trying to find meaning.

I held on to each day and made it last as long as I could. I wanted to drag the summer out for eternity. But it was coming to a close, and I was headed into a new school year. I was used to being scared to death about returning to school. But this time was different. This was a new town and a new school. Nobody knew a single thing about me. This time would be better.

My mother drove me in on the first day. We had fought about what I was going to wear that morning and the argument continued in the car.

"I told you I didn't want you wearing a shirt like that on your first day of school."

My obsession with music over the summer had found its way into my fashion sense, and I had a vast collection of rock T-shirts. Today it was an all-black short-sleeve shirt with a faded white skull on the front. I was about to make a first impression. And if I was going to reset myself, I was going to start over the way I wanted. I loved music, and I was going to show it.

"Ma, why don't you just leave me down here at the end of the street and I'll walk the rest of the way?"

"Absolutely not. I need to talk with your new principal anyway."

I sat nervously in the passenger seat and rubbed my palms over my jeans to dry the sweat and ease the tension building inside me.

We pulled up in front of the school. It was a large white structure that looked more like a giant converted barn than it did a school. It was the only junior high in the town, and it housed several grades all the way up to eighth.

Clean white sneakers and crisp new back-to-school outfits decorated the school yard. The younger kids ran around laughing and playing, while the kids my age stood in small groups with their book bags on the ground. As my mother and I went inside I felt like every eye in the yard was on me. The knot in my belly burned.

Okay, God, you helped me move here. Now please help me make it worth it.

Inside, I found my suspicion that the school was an old barn wasn't far off. Wide wooden floorboards creaked and cracked with every step. Black-painted door handles had worn to a silver shine, accentuating the best place to grip.

The principal's office was a small room. Glass covered the upper half of the wall that separated him from the hallway outside.

"Why don't you wait here?" my mother said, pointing to a chair in the hallway beneath the glass. She went inside and closed the door just as the school bell rang.

Within minutes the narrow hallway was filled with kids running, talking loudly and searching to find their rooms. I kept my head down and avoided eye contact, hoping they wouldn't notice me. My stomach ached and I braced myself, expecting someone to say something negative to me. After a while the frenzy settled down. Classroom doors closed, and the small schoolhouse became quiet again.

"Well, we've had trouble with him in the past," I heard my mother say from the thin glass behind me. "He was in the eighth grade last year, but we decided to move him back into the seventh again. I'm hoping this time around he won't do so badly."

It was true; I never was a good student. I was always more concerned about how to avoid getting beaten up than I was about who the fourteenth president of the United States was or how to multiply fractions. Now here I was, entering the eighth grade for my second time.

"I'm sure he'll do fine here, Mrs. Miller," the principal said.

"It's Tackett."

They stepped from his office, and my mother left quickly. She was running late for work.

"I'm Mr. Brosnihan, Craig, it's nice to meet you." My new principal put out his hand, and I accepted the gesture. "So you're coming from the big city, huh?"

I nodded and he led me up a wide wooden staircase with worn, creaking treads.

"You're going to like it here, Craig. I know you will," he said quietly. He opened the door to a class that was already in session. "Mr. Jameson, this is our new student, Craig Miller. He's all set to go." The principal turned back to me. "Mr. Jameson is your Homeroom teacher, your English teacher, and your Reading teacher. I'm sure this school is a lot smaller than what you are used to, but Mr. Jameson will take good care of you." He looked out at the class and smirked. "Mr. Jameson, try to behave yourself in front our new student," he joked.

Mr. Jameson looked out at the class and grabbed at his collar as if he were adjusting a tie that he wasn't wearing. "I get no respect, I tell ya," he said with dead-on Rodney Dangerfield impression. "No respect."

The class laughed and a light-hearted tone filled the room.

As much as I would have preferred to sit in the far back corner away from as many curious eyes as possible, the only seat available was right in the middle of the room. The laughter dissipated as I made my way to my seat. I could feel each person sizing me up and wondering more about me than I was of them. My stomach still ached and my face felt numb with nerves. I wanted to run out of there and never go back. I hated school. I hated the students, I hated the teachers, and I hated that I didn't belong. But my inner thoughts and the heaviness I felt were broken by Mr. Jameson's love of Rodney Dangerfield jokes.

"So you just moved here Craig?" he asked.

I nodded.

"Yeah, my parents moved a lot too when I was a kid." He paused and grabbed at his invisible tie again and spoke in his perfect Rodney voice. "But I always found them."

The class broke out into laughter, and I couldn't help but smile, too. The tension all but vanished in the presence of a teacher who knew how to read a room. The class settled into a light chatter, and I felt the tight ball in my stomach loosen a bit.

"Hey?" A voice behind me said as I was tapped on the shoulder.

I turned to see a kid behind me leaning forward.

"That's a cool shirt man," he spoke with sincerity. I thought of the argument with my mother.

"Thanks."

"You live up on Faith Avenue, right?"

"How'd you know that?"

"It's a pretty small town, in case you haven't noticed." He smiled lightly.

"Yeah, I've noticed."

"I'm Ron, by the way."

"I'm Craig."

"Yeah, I know. Listen, there's not much to see, but a bunch of us usually hang out after school, and we can show you around if you want."

I hesitated, wondering if this was some sort of a ploy to set me up and somehow make me look stupid. I did my best to bury my uneasiness. This was my chance to make a first impression-- my first and only chance to let them determine if they were going to like me or hate me. So far they had no reason to do either.

"Sure. Yeah, I can hang out."

I turned around impressed with myself for taking the risk, and from across the room I saw a smile like I had never seen before in my life. It wasn't her long blond hair or her genuine eyes. It wasn't her soft skin or breathtaking beauty. It was her smile. It was everything.

And it was a smile directed toward me.

Ron leaned forward again and patted his hand on my shoulder. "Her name is Ally," he said with a smirk.

I quickly looked away from her, and for the first time in my life, the nervous knot in my stomach wasn't there because of fear.

+++++

My memory of the day we moved flashed in my mind with strobes of light. I saw the box with my name on it, the painting, the street sign, and days at my new school. And I saw the smile of a beautiful girl. Everything happened so quickly, but I experienced each one as they appeared in the darkness with sparks of imagination.

I recalled the combined effects those events had on my life- the belief that God had listened all those years. He heard my prayers, my voice, and even my thoughts. He saved me. Things were going to change because I believed in God and He believed in me.

Then as quickly as the images had flashed and jumped before me, they began to slow. I was left in the darkness again but saturated in amazing hope. Everything was going to be okay.

9 THE HEART

I leaned against the wall of the school gymnasium in an attempt to be the farthest distance from the dance floor as possible. My stomach fluttered, and the sweat from my palms dampened my pockets. I tried to look inconspicuous, scanning the room, pretending to take in all the excitement of our eighth-grade dance, but the only thing I could focus on was Ally.

I watched beams of colored lights sweep over her face and the tiny trailing spotlights of a mirrorball highlight her eyes. She stood in a circle with other girls from our school. Their conversation appeared overly animated. Every time she laughed, she looked in my direction and allowed her smile to linger long enough for me to see it.

"She's been looking at you all night," Matt said from beside me. Matt was part of the crowd that I sometimes hung out with after school. "When are you going to ask her out?"

"She's not going to go out with me."

"Are you kidding me? It's getting ridiculous at this point. You guys have both been waiting for the other one to make a move since the first day of class. Go ask her out."

He was right. It was obvious to everyone, including me and her, that we had an interest in each other. Ever since the first day at my new school her smile captured me. A smile like I had never seen before, simply because it was intended for me. I was captivated from that very moment, held hostage by the thought of being with her. From then on, it was everything I could do to not embarrass myself every time I saw her, as I stood frozen and fixated in child-like awe.

The small-town life made it especially easy for our paths to cross. We were in the same class. A lack of stores left few places for teenagers to hang out. And come to find out, she lived right up the street from me. It seemed that wherever we went, we saw each other. For the next couple of months we played a subtle game of cat and mouse· we smiled at each other from across rooms, awkwardly passed each other in school hallways, and nervously acknowledged each other's presence in social settings. My friends pushed at me to ask her out, but the self-conscious boy in me could barely speak to her. Up until this point I had never even had a real conversation with her. Our only communication had been through eye contact and smiles. And it took everything I had to go that far. How could I ever bring myself to speak to her, especially to ask her out?

"Do you want me to do it?" Matt offered. "I'm getting sick of waiting for it myself."

The question, whether rhetorical or not, seemed like a viable solution to me for a moment. But I knew the choice was mine.

"No, I'll do it. Don't worry."

Matt rejoined a conversation with a group of other boys, expecting me to continue the delay. But I decided the game was over. I needed to be with her, and I couldn't wait any more than anyone else could.

I walked slowly across the dance floor. My stomach was weak, my mind was reeling, but my face was stone.

She watched me approach. She knew why I was coming over, and if she was nervous she hid it well. I took a deep breath to try and calm myself.

"Do you want to dance?"

"Now?" she asked with a twinge of sarcastic confusion.

Her question felt like an uppercut to my gut. *Now?* What does she mean *now?* What, she doesn't want to dance with me *now* because all these people are here. Would she be too embarrassed to be seen with me? It took more than a second for me to realize that in my determination to muster up the will to ask her to dance, I had failed to realize that no music was playing at the moment.

"Uh, well, when the music starts back up again," I said, frantically backpedaling.

Her smile turned sly with a flirtatious confidence as she saw me squirming. "What if we don't like the song?"

"Then we'll wait for another one, I guess."

"Oh, you mean I have to keep waiting?" she asked with her hands on her hips and a grin that eased my nervousness.

"No, I, um do you want to go out with me, be my girlfriend?" I couldn't believe the words just came out like that. I was shocked at my boldness but at the same time I felt relief like I had just revealed a secret that I had been dying to tell.

"Yes!"

I had never seen her smile that close up before, and it seemed even brighter and more sincere than it ever had before. She took my hand and pulled me to the dance floor just as a perfect slow song was starting up. I had no idea how to dance but I didn't care- her arms were around me, and I had never felt anything so amazing.

From that moment on, we were inseparable. I would walk the short distance up the street to her house every day after school. On the weekends we would spend all day and late into the night together. When it got too late and we had to go home, we would talk on the phone for hours, usually falling asleep with the phones still pressed against our ear.

By the end of the school year we were spending every possible moment together. Love was the only thing on my mind and when summer arrived, it was as though it had come especially for us. Its days were long and bright, and its nights were warm, quiet, and beautiful.

One night we lay in an open field. The stars sparkled with flirtatious winks as they looked down on us, and the smell of her perfume danced with a warm breeze that sent her hair trailing over my skin. I had never felt so alive, so pure, and so free. She was absolutely beautiful and soft with light blond hair and deep green eyes. She was the first light I had ever seen in a lifetime of darkness, and she loved me. To say I had fallen for her would never do it justice; I had fallen into her. Never in my life had I envisioned being accepted by someone like her, and I did everything possible to let her know it.

We were completely alone in that moment. It was only us, the warm breeze, and the night sky. She had an effortless power to distract me from the worries in my life. She freed me from the anxiety of going home and dealing with my mother and stepfather. I didn't concern myself with the fact that I hadn't seen my dad in nearly eight months because he didn't want to drive twenty miles to get me. I had buried the issues I carried with me from my past life in the city. It was just me and her and everything was perfect.

She sat up and leaned over me with a smile as warm as the night around us. "Do you think we'll be together forever?"

"I know we will," I said.

"How do you know for sure?" she asked with a sly grin, her eyes blending into the sparkling stars above us.

"I just know. I can feel it. It's one of those things you just know. Plus, I can see the future."

"Oh, really!" She pressed her lips together and looked off to the side with her eyes. "So what's going to happen next?" she asked, playfully challenging my ability.

"Well, you are going to look me in the eyes and tell me you love me, and then you'll lean in and kiss me like you never have before. And then we are going to make a promise that this will be forever."

She smiled and did exactly that.

"Promise me you'll love me forever?" she asked in a voice as soft as her kiss.

"I promise you."

She laid her head on my chest and stretched her arms around me. The sounds of a country field on a summer night echoed around us.

"See? I told you I could see the future."

+++++

The stars above us were slowly engulfed by the night, and I felt myself leaving the moment yet again. My God, no, no. Please let me stay here.

I wanted to stay forever and never wake up. The soft grass beneath me solidified into the cold, flat surface of a hospital bed. Her head against my chest transformed into cold, sticky pads pressed on my skin. I floated in the space between wakefulness and sleep, surrounded by darkness but still seeing a faint vision of her as the days seemed to fast-forward in front of me. I saw all the moments we spent together, I felt the warmth from all the times she said she loved me, and the nights we lay together beneath the stars. I saw the summer fade and the autumn set in. Dried brown leaves fell around me and each one that landed on me was another cold sticky pad pressed against my chest. The sky filled with gray clouds and the warm breeze became a cold wind.

I knew I was going out again, and I knew what was coming next. I didn't want to relive it. I shook my head, trying to make it stop and get back to the night in the field. But there was nothing I could do.

10 THE ACHE

We stood at the edge of the lake a mile from my house. There was a hidden path just off the road that led to a small clearing at the edge of the water. The clearing was nestled in a cove with a perfect view that showed just enough of the lake and shoreline that it appeared as though we were the only people in the world. It was quiet, secluded, and no one knew about it but us. There was a tall maple tree that seemed as though it had grown there on purpose. It had an angled base that made the perfect spot to sit and lean against. Carved in its bark just above where we often sat was the word *Forever.* We spent most of our time there, usually staying until the warm glow of the setting sun dissolved into the night. We were two teenagers living in the freedom of summer and learning what love could do. But summer was over now.

She stood in front of me, her eyes filled with tears. It was late autumn and a cold wind blew off the water. The once-green canopy that shaded us all summer was scattered in dried broken pieces beneath our feet. The maple tree was thickening its bark for the winter and *Forever* looked more like a scar than it did a promise. Her fingers were cold in my hands and they shook with a nervous vibration.

I knew what was coming. The words were in her eyes. They had been developing for some time now. We were about three months into our high-school freshman year, and things had grown complicated from the first day.

We had two options to choose from for high school. A school in the next town offered academic-based classes. Or we could choose a vocational school several towns away. My grades were poor and my future in an academic-type profession looked bleak. The only choice for me was to go to the vocational school. As my mother would say, I needed something "to fall back on." Swinging a hammer or turning a wrench seemed like my only options. Ally, however, was just the opposite, with a successful future clearly in her sights, and we inevitably ended up at different schools.

Though I was scared to death about being separated from her, I never told her. She was beautiful, smart, and well liked, and her personality shined. I was quiet, and awkward, and I struggled with self-confidence issues. I knew someone would take an interest in her, and she would get swept up in the sea of options before her.

From the first day they were on her--tall, good looking guys with varsity jackets and million-dollar smiles. They said all the right things and made all the right moves. I didn't have a chance against any one of them. All I could offer was a lifetime of baggage that I kept hidden behind a thin veil of fragile emotions. Within weeks I began to see other guys' phone numbers written on the wall in her room. They started calling even when I was there.

"They're just friends. Really, I love you," she would say. I believed her because she meant what she said. But as the days went on, her reassurance became less genuine.

The effect it had on me was nothing short of devastating. Despite my best efforts to leave my life in the city behind, it was still there, hanging over my head. The fear that lay dormant inside me now had reason to awaken. All it took was something like this to rattle its cage, swing open the door and let it loose. Fighting was hopeless. She was everything to me. Without her, I had nothing.

I began to make the problem worse for myself. I smothered her with insecure demands, asking her to not go anywhere without me and questioning everything she did that didn't involve me. I started to fall apart. The real me that I had worked so hard to hide began to show. I was weak, insecure, and an emotional mess. I begged her not to leave me, but I knew my time was running out.

At home things turned from bad to worse. Tension had grown to an all-time high between my step-father and me. In his eyes I was one of those teenagers who thought they knew everything. He made it his mission to knock me down every chance he got. It was as though he saw that I was falling apart and pounced on me like a hungry predator chasing the weakest in a pack of prey. But that was only the beginning.

Things really began to fall apart on a cold night in autumn. I had left my bedroom window open, hoping the chill in the air would help tame the hot flashes of anxiety. Ally was upset with me for berating her with insecure questions about her life at school, and she had not spoken with me for two days. I lay in bed with the phone under my pillow, hoping she would call and tell me everything was okay between us. I slept lightly that night, partly because of the cold chill in my room, partly because of the hard phone beneath my pillow, but mostly because I could not slow my mind from thinking. At some point I fell asleep, long enough to dream...

I stood in the tiny backyard of our house in the city. The sky was overcast. A frozen wind blew from all directions and kicked up a heavy snow. The kids I had grown up with stood side by side along the tall stockade fence that surrounded our yard: the kids who picked on me, ridiculed me, and beat me up. They stood motionless, and stared as though they were meant to kill me with their eyes.

My hands burned with cold. I looked down to see their condition, and suddenly, silently, Ally's hand took mine. I looked up to see her next to me. Her hair hardly moved in the fierce wind. Her skin appeared a golden glow like she was standing in the light of a sun that I could not see.

She stared at me with the same soft smile that lured me in that first day I saw her. For a moment I felt calm. The cold warmed slightly, but without warning my stomach balled up as if it were being strangled in an angry fist. I wheezed in pain and doubled over, holding my belly. Ally stood calmly next to me, her smile still graced. Again the pain in my belly churned. I looked down to see it moving and pulsing. My skin stretched from side to side as if a creature struggled to get out.

I doubled over again and spun in agony. The kids continued their deadly stare. I knelt in the snow gripping my stomach and doubling over again and again. My skin still stretched and bubbled. I fought to regain my strength and stand back on my feet. I lifted my head to see the small wooden door on the back of my house that led to the crawl space.

The door slowly opened. Cobwebs stretched from the thin wooden slats and tore as it opened further. Ally stood next to me motionless, her yellow glow casting a beam of light into the dark room. Specks of dust floated, shining like tiny diamonds in the light. From the darkness came a hand, a dry, dirty, calloused hand. The fingers bent sharply.

I stood still, empty of all strength while the cold wind scraped across my body. I could not run. I could not move backwards. I could not even find the will to want to. I reached through the yellow beam of light and took the hand that called for me from the darkness of the crawlspace. I felt the hair on the knuckles and felt the long fingernails. I felt the strength, the ugliness, and all of its dark intentions.

It pulled me into the room. I looked back to see Ally, beautiful and smiling. I wanted to stop. I wanted to let go of the hand and run out, but I couldn't. The will was not in me. I felt only a numbing, breathtaking fear. Tears streamed from my eyes, and my belly boiled. Suddenly the door slammed shut with a force so heavy, it woke me from my sleep.

My eyes opened with a burst of fear. I gasped for air. A billowy cloud of breath blew in front of me in the cold autumn air that filled my bedroom. I sat up in a panic, and tried to shake myself from the dream. I grasped my stomach, expecting to find a writhing beast trying to claw its way out.

I looked around my room and saw the black velvet painting of Jesus on my wall. All at once, panic-stricken, I realized I had forgotten to keep my promise to God. I had lost myself in my new life. I hadn't prayed every day like I said I would. I hadn't given credit to God or remembered to talk with Him. I hadn't even acknowledged the painting on my wall. I owed God, and my problems with Ally were His method of collecting on what I owed. He had moved me from the city and saved me from the overpowering hands of Ben, He had taken me from the schoolyard battlefield, and He had given me the opportunity to know what love felt like. Now, He was fed up with being pushed to the back of the line.

I fell to my knees before the painting. I was filled with regret. "God, I am sorry.... I am sorry.... I am so sorry." My words came directly from my heart. I meant what I said. I was truly sorry. I was never so ashamed and so scared, everything was my fault.

I was breaking down. The last fifteen years of my life had caught up to me, and my mind was crumbling. I felt emotions that ranged from regret to fear and remorse to guilt. Begging for mercy, I was plagued with doubt that I was sorry only because things had gone wrong, that my guilt with God was only because I was lost and broken. I believed God saw this, too, and I imagined him looking upon me in disappointment.

It was a moment I will never forget-- a moment that became the initial surfacing of a lifetime of pent-up emotion, confusion, and pain, a moment when I started to fall apart from the inside out.

The thought of God's disappointment in me never abated. Despite how irrational it may have sounded, even to me, I could do nothing to dismiss it. My God was a good

God, a forgiving God. He loved and helped me. He held the clouds still and let me spin the world. He believed in me because I believed in Him. Although it didn't make any sense, the thought of Him as a debt collector embedded itself within me. Each day I was consumed with a sense of guilt and regret. I promised God I would do whatever He wanted and repay Him for everything He had done for me. I went through my day feeling as though I was being constantly observed. I imagined him holding a hammer over my head, waiting for me to do something wrong, ready to crush my existence.

I don't know what really happened, I don't know how my thoughts got so caught up in it, and I don't know why I believed God held my life in the balance and my feet to the fire. Maybe it was because of all the issues I grew up with had finally surfaced and my mind began to fall apart. Maybe it was because I spent nearly every day of my childhood in fear, begging my miseries to stop. Or maybe I blamed myself for the things that happened under the house and my mother's violent outbursts. Maybe I thought I wasn't good enough for my father to take the time to see me. I really don't know. But I do know that the feeling was there, and I was incapable of controlling it. It came fast and hard and it seemed so real, it consumed me completely.

I believed that God was judging my every move. But somewhere within me, a very small part of me knew that He would never do that. I knew that what I was feeling was crazy. The confusion continued to grow until one day, I lost all control.

I walked home from the bus stop after school on an October afternoon. My head hung heavy and my eyes stared at the ground in front of my feet. The hood of my black sweatshirt covered my head and gave me a false sense of seclusion from the rest of the world. I wondered if while at school Ally had been swayed any closer toward leaving me. I turned up the volume in headphones and tried to distract myself. I searched for solace in the words, but each line matched exactly with what I felt, and the music only made things worse. With my head hung low and my eyes staring at the ground, I saw a scrap of white paper blow across the ground in front of me.

They say that when a person is in a car accident, a million thoughts race through their mind all within a split second. They are able to see the situation in its entirety, formulate a plan, and even foresee the outcome of different scenarios all before the moment of impact. I believe without doubt that it is true, and for me, stepping on a piece of paper on an October afternoon at fifteen years old was the equivalent of a highway pile-up.

My momentum pulled me forward, one foot in front of the other, unstoppable. The piece of paper skipped across the pavement, unaware of the danger. My foot hung in the air and time slowed. As I braced myself for collision, my thoughts battled one another.

Don't step on it! Look, it's white, it's pure, and it's innocent. Crushing it would be wrong. Is that what you want, to break things apart and make them worse than they are? I thought you wanted things to be better. I thought you wanted Ally to love you and stay with you. Every muscle tightened as I tried to stop my foot from skidding forward.

Keep it pure. Keep it perfect.

But it's a piece of paper on the side of the road. It's meaningless and insignificant.

You are on the side of the road with it. Does that make you meaningless and insignificant? If you crush this paper then everything else in your life will crumble along with it.

That's ridiculous. This paper has nothing to do with my life.

How do you know? How do you know that this paper

wasn't sent here in front of you as a test to see if you really cared about your life and what happens next? How do you know that if you crush this piece of paper everything you love and care about will not be destroyed with it?

Because that makes no sense. It is only paper on the street. It is just trash.

Do you really want to test it?

No, no, my God no. I don't want to take the risk of anything bad happening. I don't want to test it. I won't step on it.

But it was hopeless. I was already in motion. My foot was already taking the step, and the paper lay beneath it. I saw my shoe crash to the ground and crush an innocent, pure, white piece of paper. And with it, my whole life shattered.

Panic set in, but in the same instant, an equal and opposite feeling tried to take hold-- the rational thought that this truly was just a piece of paper, and what the hell was I thinking? But I was powerless to give it credence. The potential of significance behind the collision was too real, and I was too unwilling to gamble with another bad thing in my life.

I had to stop. I had to fix the situation, the broken paper, the horrific destruction that I had caused. I wanted to keep walking, but I could not. I was compelled to stop. I picked up the paper, uncrumpled it, and pressed the pure white sheet between my hands. I had to make things better again. I had to make sure nothing bad would happen.

But the damage was done. The paper was ruined. With one careless step I had changed my own destiny. For the rest of my walk home, I was filled with the anxious compulsive need to stop and pick up every single piece of trash on the side of the road. If I picked it up, and if I showed the trash care and love, maybe it would make up for the pain I had caused to the piece of paper. Maybe it would change my fate and cancel out whatever bad thing I had caused.

None of it made sense to me. I knew this delusion wasn't real, but no matter how hard I tried, I couldn't stop feeling it. And for some reason God was at the center of it. I felt He was testing me to see if I would do these things to keep my life in order, and if I didn't, he would let things fall apart even worse than they had.

Before long, everything I did revolved around these thoughts.

The compulsions started with the papers on the ground. I would pick up every piece of litter or trash I saw. If I tried to step over it, the knowledge that something bad would happen stopped me in my tracks. I had no choice but to pick it up. Move forward and suffer, or stop and pick it up and save myself. That was how it worked. Succumb to the compulsion or pay dearly with an unknown consequence. I would get home from school with my pockets bulging with trash.

If I thought I should shut the light off in my room, I had to do it, even if I needed it on. Then I would get the feeling that I hadn't shut it off *right* and needed to do it again. I was held hostage for hours in front of a light switch turning it on and off until I felt I had done it *right*. I didn't tell anyone about it. I thought that God was testing me, and part of the deal between him and me was keeping my mouth shut.

The inner turmoil destroyed my fragile armor. Once more, I became the scared little boy who had lain in the dirt beneath his house and hidden under the covers while his home was turned upside-down.

How could I expect Ally to love me and want to be with me? She was beautiful. She was smart and she glowed with an incredible brightness. Above all, she was free. I could never hold her down or keep her from living the life of popularity and glamour that was unfolding all around her.

I met her beside the lake as she had asked. I knew why she wanted to meet, but I couldn't believe it was happening. She stood in front of me with tears dripping down her cheeks. Her hands nervously shook in mine, and the cold wind off the water shuffled the dead leaves around our feet. She didn't have to say a word. Her eyes told me everything. It was over. I stared at the ground, hoping it was a dream. I couldn't look at her face. I couldn't watch her tell me what I knew she was about to say.

"I can't do this anymore." Her voice softened as if she could hear my heart breaking. "Everything is too complicated."

I wanted to stop her. I wanted to drop to my knees and beg her not to leave me. I wanted to make a million promises about how I was going to change and how I could give her so much more than anyone else ever could. But I knew that wasn't true. I knew I had nothing to offer.

I loved her from the first moment I saw her. I loved her for every day we had spent together and for every night we watched the sun set and the stars shine. I loved her for every moment she touched my face and whispered she loved me. And in the end, I loved her enough to let her leave.

"I'll never forget our promise," she whispered. "I will love you forever, and I will never forget you for the rest of my life. But I just can't be with you anymore."

My eyes filled with tears as her words sank deep within me and buried themselves within my heart. I stood there, alone again, slowly breaking apart with the dry autumn leaves that crushed beneath her feet as she walked away.

+++++

The memory faded. I felt no physical sensation and heard no sounds. I was only left with the emotion of terrible heartache and the somber thought of how bad it hurt. I lay weak and broken. If my soul could cry, it would have.

I floated in the darkness suspended between the emotional pain of my memories and the physical pain of waking up. In this moment, saturated in the memory of a broken heart, I had a brief realization of all that was happening to me. I recalled the memories I had already relived and began to see the significance in each one and the changes they brought about in me throughout my life. I knew that I was living my life over again through a series of dreams and flashes. I recognized the pain in my nose and throat were from a tube and I heard the faint sounds of a heart monitor and a busy hospital. But I was too weak to stay awake. My heart was too heavy and my mind exhausted. The memory of the day my heart broke lingered in the air around me and I lost the fragile grip I had on my awareness.

11 THE FRIEND

"Step on a crack, break your mother's back." The words chanted uncontrollably through my mind with every step I took. I inhaled with a heavy, conscious effort, to try and calm the anxiety and confusion inside me. My feet ached from the tension of contorted muscles. Each step became an ever-growing struggle to avoid a web of broken lines that ran through the concrete of the back country road. It was getting dark, and the cracks in the road looked like they had been drawn with charcoal in the fading daylight.

"Step on a crack, break your mother's back." *God, this isn't real.*

With each slow, steady, and calculated step, a vibrating wave of needles ran down the back of my neck.

The tap of my shoe resembled the snap of bone, the grinding of cartilage, and my mother's pleading screams.

Relax. Look up. Look straight ahead. The cracks don't matter. This makes no sense.

I stepped forward, balancing on an invisible wire, walking through a loaded minefield, and teetering on the edge of a thousand-foot drop.

One step at a time. Avoid the lines.

It had only been a few months since Ally left me, and the intrusive thoughts that had started around that time had now consumed me. I suffered from major depression, constant anxiety, and a debilitating, irrational fear. I had withdrawn completely. I spoke to very few people and spent my time outside of school either locked in my room or several towns away at my friend Dylan's house.

Dylan and I had met at school a couple months before. We clicked right way. My summer spent alone after our move to the country had left me with a passion for song lyrics and a love for music. Dylan obviously shared that love. We both had long hair and an arsenal of concert T-shirts. It was also obvious that we both had some issues. But for everything we had in common, there was just as much that we didn't.

When Ally left, it changed me inside. She had broken me so badly that I knew I couldn't survive another blow like that. And although I was fragile and frail on the inside, my external defenses hardened for the first time. The anger in me surfaced. It all happened in a heartbeat one day in high school shop class.

Every class has an arrogant, loudmouth kid who feels he has something to prove. In my class it was Alex. Alex was a tall, jock type with a tough attitude. He had been stalking me from the first day, eyeing my meek and self-conscious demeanor. Every time I looked in his direction, he was staring at me, always with an intense threatening glare as if he was sizing me up. Once we made eye contact, he usually barked a loud, "What the fuck are you looking at?" hoping everyone else would hear how tough he was.

I did my best to ignore him, but I was reaching the end of my rope. I hadn't been picked on since the days in the city. And with all I had done to try and leave that part of my life behind, I wasn't about to get bullied again. But still I kept to myself, and hoped he would leave me alone.

We were in our carpentry shop class one afternoon. Two dozen kids from different grades and backgrounds mixed together and spread out over the large room. It was a near perfect real-life industrial setting. Huge saws buzzed, nail guns popped, and pneumatic presses hissed all around the room. On this day it was my job to man the tool crib- a responsibility that no one wanted, but each student had to take turns doing. As tool crib attendant, we had to sit in a room full of all the portable tools for the shop: hammers, clamps, screw guns, etc., and get each student what they wanted. It was also the attendant's responsibility to make sure they returned it all in good working order at the end of the day. It was a degrading job that mixed "water boy" with "hall monitor."

For several hours I doled out tools to inconsiderate kids who treated me like their personal butler. All the while I battled the compulsive thoughts that tore into my mind and hoped no one would notice: I counted the holes in the peg board, straightened the tools that hung around the room, and traced lines in the floor with my fingertip.

I looked up to see Alex strutting toward me, and I knew from his demeanor that he was looking for trouble. He stood in the doorway of the tool crib with an intimidating stance and glared at me. "Get me an extension cord," he commanded.

The extension cords in our shop were industrialized with a thick, black rubber coating nearly an inch in diameter. On the ends were large, heavy metal boxes with four outlets in them. I ignored his attitude and reached back to get him one of the cords.

Before my hand reached it, compulsive thoughts attacked me. This time they told me to hold the cord in my grip with all four fingers evenly spaced around it. That would symbolize balance and help me to avoid something bad from happening. I knew it was ridiculous, but I wasn't about to contest the feeling, especially with Alex standing right behind me.

I reached for the cord, my hand extended, flattened with my fingers spread wide, ready for the task. My palm pressed against the black rubber surface. I folded my fingers at the first set of knuckles.

Get it right, slowly, do not make a mistake.

My fingers, carefully spread to an even distance, folded the rest of the way around the cord one knuckle at a time.

Everything is in good order. You may proceed. Wait, your thumb! There is no balance with your thumb involved: four evenly spaced fingers on one side and a bent thumb on the other. Four against one. If you pick up this cord, whatever tragedy is in your future will be four times greater, four times harder, and four times more painful. Maybe after school, maybe next week, maybe when you least expect it, but it will come, and it be swift and severe. No one will help you. Four against one.

I instantly retracted my grip, hoping to stop the progression of my thoughts, but the energy was still on the cord. When I had incorrectly placed my hand around it, I created an imbalance. When I pulled my hand away so quickly, I did nothing to fix the problem. *I must put my hand back on the cord the same way it was and then retract it in the exact reverse order with the intention of removing the imbalance.*

That's the only way. It must be done.

My stomach sank, and a flash of heat spread up the back of my neck. I took a deep breath and tried to clear away the fear building in my mind. My arm stretched out, my palm pressed against the cord, my fingers evenly bent at the first set of knuckles. The heat continued crawling over my scalp, around my ears, and down onto my forehead.

Hold it the exact way you had it before, then let it go in the perfect reverse order.

"Give me the fucking cord," Alex commanded again from behind me.

Goddammit! Please just pick up the cord. Please just leave me alone and let me pick up this stupid, fucking, insignificant extension cord.

Reverse the order, slowly, as you did when you gripped it the first time.

"Give me the fucking cord, or I'll shove it up your ass." Alex's frustration was boiling over. He had a problem with me to begin with, but now he was getting ready to do something about it.

My knuckles straightened, one section at a time, bending upward, relieving the pressure of my fear. My thumb pulled back slowly, and my palm was just about to come off the cord.

"Are you fucking kidding me? Give me the fucking cord!" Alex yelled out.

One more time, and I could do it. One more time, and I can pick it up. My body buzzed with anxiety and tension. I wanted to scream and tear the cord into a million pieces, I wanted to rip my hair out and scream, but my thoughts kept me in their grip.

Reach for it again, with balance. One finger and one thumb?

No, your thumb is bigger than your finger. There is no balance in that.

One thumb and two fingers?

Definitely not.

Goddammit, just let me pick up the fucking cord! I stood frozen while a battle waged in my mind.

"Get the fuck out of my way!" Alex rushed forward and pushed me aside with his shoulder. He reached for the cord and snatched it up with one quick jerk. He swung it so hard and fast that the metal box on the end lashed around like a bullwhip. And before I could react, before I even noticed what was happening, the large, jagged metal box blindsided me with a left hook and smashed me in the mouth.

At first I saw only black, then red, and then I saw everything. I saw the girls who crowded around me in elementary school while my back was pressed against the wall. I saw the trail of blood left in the snow from a fist to my nose. I saw a blue Styrofoam tray in front of me while I ate alone at a lunchroom table. And I saw every opening I had to land my punches on a high-school bully who had pushed things too far.

My mind focused on my fist. My knuckles bent sharply at all points. My fingers evenly aligned. Everything was in good balance. And for the first time in my life, I let my anger go like a flaming arrow from a fully drawn bow. I don't recall hitting him. I only saw him fall. And I didn't make a conscious decision to continue; my fists fell on their own and rained down on him with the force of hailstones while he desperately tried to cover his head.

Alex was caught off guard. He didn't know what was going on inside me. He didn't expect to be attacked so hard. And no matter how hard he hit me first, he didn't deserve the years of pent-up anger that I brought down on him.

The deep trance of the moment was broken by a shop teacher charging me like a football linebacker, driving his shoulder into my stomach and lifting me off the floor. He pressed my body against the wall. "What the hell are you doing?"

My eyes darted around the room, trying to clear the images from my mind and focus on the reality of the stunned crowd that had formed in front of us. Alex moaned on the floor, still covering his head.

It didn't take long for word to spread and a reputation

to form. I had reached a new level in myself that allowed me to protect what little piece of self-esteem I had left. I was still as fragile as ever, but I had gained enough confidence to harden my shell. On the outside I appeared the opposite of the meek boy who took all those punches and got spit on growing up. I had found my anger and my defense.

In contrast, my friend Dylan was extremely timid, and not through any fault of his own. A year or so before high school, he was at an industrial park trying out a new skateboard he had gotten for his birthday. The park was a great place to skate with smooth blacktop and all kinds of obstacles, so at times it was a popular hangout and drew a very mixed crowd. Dylan was there only a short time when a carload of guys pulled in and wanted to try his board. There were four of them in their early twenties and obviously either drunk or on drugs. Dylan reluctantly let one of them try it out, and the guys began sharing his board and tearing it up pretty bad. When he stepped in to get it back, they started beating him. This was a slow and methodical beating. They passed the skateboard to one another, taking turns smashing him in the head.

Dylan's dad found him unconscious on the pavement. The assailants were long gone. Dylan spent several days in the hospital. The whole thing shook him up so badly, he changed completely. He was in a constant state of fear, afraid of just about everything. He wouldn't make eye contact with people. I once saw him duck below the windows in his house as he passed by because he was too scared to look outside. His fear was irrational and uncontrollable. In fact, it was just like mine except his was on the outside.

The worst part about Dylan's fear was that it didn't suit him. It didn't fit in with the rest of who he was, like a separate entity that bullied him around. The real Dylan hid in the corner of his personality. The real Dylan was fun, lighthearted, and funny, even hilarious at times. He had a peculiar personality all his own and could make people laugh by pretty much doing nothing at all. He made goofy faces and talked in silly voices. He even had his own language from renaming common objects. He called cigarettes *wigs* and soda, *dune*. He had a fun-loving innocence about him that I never found in anyone else. His innocence made my sympathy for his suffering even stronger.

Although I was an emotional mess ready to break under the slightest pressure, I thought nothing of sticking up for him even when the odds were severely stacked against me. His timid nature made him an easy target early-on in the school year when all the tough guys were trying to establish their position. I took it seriously when someone singled him out, and it broke my heart to see him scared. I knew that feeling all too well. It was like a trigger to me, and I ended up learning how to stand up for myself by standing up for him.

We became close almost immediately, and we opened up to each other about everything. I told him all about my compulsive thoughts and how overpowering they were. He never judged me and he became the only person I could talk to about it.

Our love for music brought us even closer, and it gave me the outlet I so desperately needed. Dylan had a guitar that his mother bought him at a yard sale. He had an incredible natural ability to play. He could mimic just about any song on the radio without ever having a single lesson.

For me the passion for music was all about the words. Lyrics were what had me so fascinated. Since the summer that we moved, I had started writing my own. I heard melodies in my head constantly. Sometimes I would hear an entire song, music and all, playing in the back of my mind. The words flowed at times without any thought. I wrote them down as often as I could. And more often than not, I wrote on the scraps of paper that I picked up from the side of the road in my frequent attempts to save my life. It was my way of giving purpose to pieces of discarded trash.

Dylan became my confidant through it all. I started to spend more time at his house than I did at my own. He had a dilapidated garage in his backyard that was in the far back corner of the yard, away from the house. A wooded area blocked it from the rest of the neighborhood. Dylan and I spent all of our time together in there. It was a unique structure that looked like a cross between an oversized garage and a two-story barn. It stood on a thick granite foundation and was about four hundred square feet. A boarded up section of an exterior wall looked like it had been the entry way to a carport at one time. The only way in or out was a wooden door much like the entrance to a house, but the window in the top half was broken with an old piece of paneling nailed over it. The top hinge had broken off, which made it permanently stuck in the open position.

When you're as troubled inside as Dylan and I were, there is something in you that wants the hurt to be seen. A part of you that needs something solid and tangible to reflect the pain you feel. For us, an old, dilapidated garage summed up our entire world. And just like us, the more you looked inside, the more you realized how distressed the garage really was.

The beams that once held the floor solid had badly rotted in random places. The uneven boards made the entire surface look like something you might find in an amusement-park funhouse. A poorly constructed set of stairs, loosely nailed together, went up to the second floor where we spent most of our time. The floorboards up there were shoddy and missing in certain sections, making holes that went through to the first floor. The walls and ceiling had no interior finish work, and the nails from the siding and roof shingles broke through the plywood, surrounding us in a fully spiked enclosure.

Dylan's parents were good people. We were two troubled teenage boys who wanted to be left alone, and they gave us all the freedom we needed. They were very sympathetic toward Dylan's issues and his fears, and they had a general idea of what I was going through. They saw the connection we had and never questioned the amount of time I spent there. Because of my mother and stepfather's views on children, they didn't have any problem with me not being home much, either. I began taking Dylan's bus home from school instead of mine and not going home for days.

We spent all of our time together up in the garage. We

cleaned it up and made it into a place where we could hang out, feed our obsession with music, and hide from the world.

And hiding was all I wanted to do. I wished I could run and bury myself in the corner of the darkest shadows. Hide away from the world around me, away from the fear that plagued me, and away from the overpowering thoughts that invaded my mind. Especially now, as I tried to walk down a broken country road with a million painful lines spread across its surface.

Each step was a nightmare come true. Each time I stretched forward my thoughts grew more intense, the fear overwhelmingly real. "Step on a crack, break your mother's back." I balanced, swaying in the breeze of the evening as darkness consumed the daylight.

Tiptoe.

One step at a time.

This isn't real. This isn't real. My face tense with concentration.

Try to change it. Try to make it go away. "Step on a crack, break your mother's back." The imaginary sound of snapping, cracking, and jagged scrapes of bone screeched inside of me. *God, make this go away! Make it stop, please.*

Just a few more steps and a clearing in the road. Just a few more tight, rigid, and perfectly calculated steps, and I will be free from the web of shattered concrete.

My heart punched at my chest, my lungs shook inside me, and my head pulsed with maddening pressure.

I fought to distract myself. I fought for anything normal and rational. I tried to pretend I was okay and everything was fine. God, I hated it! I hated it so bad. *Please make it all stop.*

My last step. Relief, a break in the moment.

I was through. Night had fallen. For nearly an hour I had been crossing a section of broken road no more than twenty feet long. I sat on the side of the road with my head in my hands, trying to make sense of what had been happening. I tried to gather myself and listen to the rational thoughts that fought to crawl through the dense underbrush of fear and anxiety. I listened for anything that would make sense to me: feelings, answers, words.

I searched my stuffed pockets for a piece of scavenged scrap paper big enough to write on. I flattened it against my leg, and with a pen I kept with me always, I began to write whatever needed to come.

I don't remember when I started to fall
But I know that I will never come back
Because I can't climb out of an endless hole
Wrapped in bricks from an unwanted past
And I never said that I wanted to be
So I'll keep counting down through my days
And wait for an end to set me free
From a world of all I hate.

+++++

My hand continued to write as the pen and paper dissolved away and the darkness of the night quickly set in. The street light, the trees, and the cracked country road all disappeared, and all I was left with was the weight of the words that poured from me that night. I remembered the desperate need to let them out and the relief I got when the pen moved over the paper. I tried to continue writing and get everything out. My hand struggled to move in the grasp of the leather strap. Suddenly, a stranger's voice spoke calmly in the darkness. "You're going to be okay. We're here to help. Just try to relax."

I felt someone take my hand as I moved an imaginary pen over invisible paper. They pressed their palm firmly into mine to stop the shaking. "Everything's okay, we're here to help you," the voice repeated.

My hand steadied. I thought of Dylan. I thought of how incredible it felt to have a friend who understood and cared. I missed him. I wished I could open my eyes and see the stranger, but I somehow knew it didn't matter. All that did matter was that someone cared enough to hold my hand and let me know they were there.

12 THE PAIN

I stood in the corner of a makeshift medical exam room under bright fluorescent lights, wearing only my underwear. My hands hung by my side with swollen knuckles and open sores. Long, thin lines of open skin trailed across my arms, chest, and stomach. My eyes were bloodshot and heavy, and my head ached from the pressure in my ears and sinuses. My teeth were clenched as if my jaw were wired shut. I tried to swallow, but my mouth being so dry it made it impossible. A tall man with broad shoulders stood guard next to the door ready to stop any attempt I made at leaving. It was late, half past midnight, and I had just arrived after a two-hour trip from Massachusetts to a psychiatric hospital in New Hampshire, where I was being admitted.

It had only been a few short months since the incident on the back country road and my self-control had been deteriorating with the gray skies of the passing winter. Keeping myself together became increasingly difficult. My behavior had progressed far beyond things like picking up trash, flipping light switches, and avoiding cracks in the ground. I found myself having to do all kinds of compulsive acts. They were both ritualistic and random.

I woke every morning with a need to open one eye at a time, first left, then right. If I forgot or did it wrong, something bad was going to happen, and I spent the next twenty-four hours saturated in a gut-wrenching worry until the next morning gave me a chance to correct it. I spun my schoolbooks around a certain number of times before I opened them. The number of times changed at random. I did it until it felt right.

I had a commanding need to count everything: my footsteps as I walked, tiles in the ceiling, and cars on the street. I even counted my words as I spoke. Some nights I sat up until three in the morning and counted holes in the screen of my bedroom window. The baseline to everything was that if I did the compulsion right, then God would keep a bad thing from happening; if I did it wrong, then a life-changing horror was sure to come.

All day, every day, I was plagued with the fear I had grown up with. The same fear as when I worried about what Ben was going to do next, or what the kids were going to do to me when I got to school and what my mother's mood would be like and how she would express it. But this fear was much more powerful. This fear didn't just tie knots in my stomach, it tied knots in my mind. And on one night in particular, I couldn't get them untangled.

It was mid-winter. There had been a long break in the snowfall and the air was unusually warm. The skies were a clear, beautiful dark-blue with green diamond accents. I lay in the field where Ally and I had spent so many summer nights.

My back pressed flat against the frost-hardened ground. The soft green grass that once stood tall with life now lay frail, brown, and lifeless, stripped of its beauty by the dry winter air. I tried to imagine the nights when Ally and I would lie there together, her head on my chest and her comforting arms around me. I tried to remember a day when everything was perfect, when I could feel her touch, smell her hair, and hear her voice.

I lay alone, trying to bring the memories closer, trying to navigate them through a tangled mess of overpowering, intrusive thoughts.

I looked up at the same stars that were with us when we once lay together, the stars that watched when we kissed and listened when we promised. My heart still broke to think of her.

"Star light, star bright, first star I see tonight. I wish I may, I wish I might, have the wish I wish tonight," I whispered hoping so much to be heard. But almost immediately my thoughts cracked apart with a nervous explosion through my body.

First star you see? That wasn't the first star you saw! You chose which ever you pleased and decided it was the one you would make a wish on. It wasn't the first. You chose it randomly. You've created disorder even in the celestial sky-- disorder in the sky, disorder in the world, and disorder in the lives of whoever looks at the night sky.

No! Stop!

Fix it! Fix it now! Find the first star you saw tonight and begin again.

There is nothing wrong with what I have done!

My mind spun in orbital confusion, trying to grasp a

rational, stable solution.

Nothing is wrong with what I did!

Fix it! Find the first star.

My eyes darted around the sky. I saw a faint blinking dot just above the tree line. Was that it?

One!

A bright green glow a few inches above. I don't know.

Two!

Several lined up in a straight line. I can't remember. God, please!

Three! Four! Five! Six!

Please stop counting. Please just let me go.

I fought wildly inside and tried to slow the progression of my thoughts as they steamrolled through my mind, overlapping one another and intertwining themselves. But I was powerless, tied in a restraining grasp of irrationality. The counting continued from one blinking star to another. I searched an entire sky of tiny dancing lights to find the first one that my eyes had seen that night, hours before. My face and hands were numb, and my lungs struggled to expand. The pressure was overwhelming as I fell apart from the inside out.

It took everything I had to break the trance, reclaim my eyes from the sky, and fight the fear that was crushing me. I rose from the ground and ran across a dry, dead, frosted earth.

I was alone, not in the moment, but in everything. I had no one to help me. I had tried several times to tell my mother what was going on and she discounted me saying, "Everyone has things like that that they do." Despite how much I pressed her, she still would not listen. "They're idiosyncrasies. I have things like that, too," she'd say.

She had even watched me get stuck in a trance a few times and laughed about it. Once, I spent over twenty minutes straightening out a pair of shoes that I had left on the stairs in our house. By the time it felt like I had done it well enough, I was sweating with anxiety and frustration. My mother stood at the top of the stairs and shook her head with a grin, not having the slightest idea of what I had just gone through.

I knew she didn't understand, and tonight was not the night to try and convince her again. It was late, and she had been drinking. If I went to her now in a panic, having a nervous breakdown, who knew where it would end up.

I ran as fast as I could all way to my house. I closed my bedroom door and called my brother, Tyler. He answered the phone, and the second I heard his voice I instantly fell apart. "Tyler, I don't know how to say this, I don't know where to even start, but I need help. I need someone to help me. I don't know what's happening, Tyler." The words were hard to say. My chest tightened as the anxiety continued attacking me in an effort to stifle my words.

"I don't have control over my mind, and I feel like something else is controlling it," I said. "Mom won't help me. She won't help me, Tyler. I don't know what to do."

"Brother?" his voice resonated with shock. "I'll take care of you. I'm going to help you. It's okay."

We stayed on the phone for hours while he listened to everything I said. I told him about the painting in my room, about my deal with God and that I failed to hold up my end of the bargain. I told him about my thoughts and how they were polluted with ridiculous commands and threatening fears. And I told him about how scared I was that I might not be able to control it much longer.

The next day he called my mother and had a long conversation with her that was based somewhere along the lines of, "If you don't help him, I will."

A week or so later she brought me to a psychiatrist who determined I had an anxiety disorder, severe depression, and obsessive compulsive disorder. "The OCD is based in a chemical imbalance in your brain," he said, "probably brought on by a growth spurt. The anxiety and depression are the residual effects of the OCD."

He never asked me about my past or searched to find the root cause of my issues. Instead he prescribed me a concoction of medications and set me up to meet with a counselor once a week.

I was desperate for help and open to any and all suggestions. I took my pills with discipline and never missed an appointment, but nothing worked.

The counselor and I weren't exactly on the same page, which I don't think helped much, either. He was very shy and reserved and seemed to be more nervous than me at times. I was uncomfortable talking with him about the issues from my childhood. I avoided subjects of my past and he never tried to probe. I was, however, coming at him with all kinds of complex issues regarding my OCD, anxiety, and suicidal thoughts. He focused on my breathing as a way to help. He spent the majority of our one-hour sessions teaching me breathing exercises to tame my anxiety.

I was crying myself to sleep every night with a knife to my wrist and making negotiations with God throughout my entire day, and he worried about my breathing! Needless to say, we had a major disconnection between us, and I never felt comfortable letting our conversations get too deep.

Despite the best efforts of the doctors and the effects of the medication, things got worse. New rituals and random thoughts filled each day. I kept a piece of paper with me to track all the ones I got right versus all the ones I got wrong. At the end of the day, I tallied them up to see if I passed God's tests.

My compulsions continued to become more and more out of hand. I had to walk up the steps of the school bus a certain way: each foot needed to be evenly spaced between the lines that were painted on the steps. Sometimes I would have to get off the bus and repeat the process.

The bus driver looked at me like I was crazy. "What the hell are you doing? Get in the bus!" None of the kids said anything to me about it or gave me a hard time. I'm sure it had something to do with my character. By this time my internal turmoil had started to show on the outside. I dressed in black every day and was so in love with music that my headphones never left my ears. I kept a pen with me always and a pocket stuffed with my scavenged scrap paper. I took them out whenever the need to write came on and started scribbling anywhere at any time, as if I was receiving the most important message of my life. My hair was long and hung in my face. I was extremely defensive and didn't allow anyone to make me feel worse than I already did. At that time, however, I believed that people left me alone because I kept my feet perfectly spaced between the lines on the school bus.

Dylan was the only one who really understood me. And though nobody said anything to me directly, they were beginning to talk about me, and Dylan was sticking up for me as much as I was for him. I spent as much time as possible at his house away from my parents and away from the small town.

On the afternoon before my hospital admittance, I took Dylan's bus home from school and planned to spend the weekend with him. It had been an especially difficult week for me. My OCD was taking on a life of its own. I had been keeping track of my score and following how many compulsions I had satisfied. But a new compulsion had developed. It forced me to avoid the number three and any multiple of it. It turned into a ritualistic thing that imbedded itself into everything I did. I couldn't use sentences with three words or six words or nine.... I couldn't do anything that required three movements such as, (1) reach for a doorknob, (2) turn it, (3) open the door. The list was endless. The difficulty, aside from managing it, was keeping track of it all.

I was counting words in my mind as I spoke to people, while, at the same time, counting the movements I made. Then I would start counting the number of exchanges in the conversation. It continued on and on, and I found myself even beginning to count the number of times the subject of the conversation changed.

The number of things I was counting also needed to be measured. Each tally and the fearful thought that motivated it layered on top of one another. I was riddled with lists of numbers sounding off in my mind while continuously trying to avoid any multiple of three. On top of it all, I was plagued with unimaginable fear that if I made even the slightest mistake, something devastating would happen.

I was in the garage with Dylan and trying to tally up my score card for the day. The numbers compulsion came on as I tried to write. It folded itself around my mind like a python squeezing the life from its prey. My mind strained to focus on a hundred things at once: the folds in the paper, the numbers scattered across it, how many fingers I was using to hold it. Thoughts grew like roots and sprouted new-erratic ideas. I fought to keep up with all of them. I knew that everything I was doing was irrational and unnecessary, but I was powerless to stop it. I felt possessed. I had no control over my mind anymore. It was running itself freely into madness, and I could only stand by as the victim, fearing that any mistake would have dire consequences for me.

My heart pounded in my chest, my soul shattered, and my spirit collapsed. I was done appeasing my illness. I couldn't take it anymore. I was tired of living a life of fear and silent suffering. I had lived my whole life as a victim of other people, and now I was a victim of my own self. I was breaking, and everything was falling down around me. Nobody knew what I felt inside. Nobody helped me, nobody saw me. How the hell could you not *see* me? I've been a broken mess screaming out for help my whole life-- my whole fucking life!

My fists tightened around the pen. My emotions

fueled the strength in my muscles. I scratched the pen back and forth across a paper full of numbers as if I were etching stone with a chisel. The paper tore to shreds. I stabbed the pen into the floor and punched the wall. "Leave me the fuck alone!" *One! Two!* My OCD began counting my punches in the background of my mind. My knuckles burst open. Blood splashed across my fingers. *Three!*

The world around me rushed in, streaking across my eyes. Tears blurred my vision. I began reliving a day in the life of my childhood. I was under the house getting raped by a mentally challenged, deaf man. I was at school getting picked on for being molested. The teachers were giving me a hard time because I was a sloppy kid with bad grades. I was kneeling on my bedroom floor while my stepfather berated me until I cried.

I hated my mother for not seeing it. I hated my stepfather for fucking with me--a little boy, a five, six, seven, eight, nine, ten-year-old boy. You son of a bitch!

Four! My fists stung and swelled. My face turned numb, and my lungs burned as if I was breathing in a frozen arctic wind.

I hated my father for not being there for me, never

caring, never giving me a minute of his fucking time, for walking away and wiping his hands of responsibility, as his son sat on the front steps for half his life waiting to see his dad again.

Five!

My OCD, my anxiety, my depression, the overwhelming thoughts that plagued me, all came rushing in as a united army attacking me from all sides. *Six! Seven!* My mind continued counting punches as the fear of punching wrong or counting wrong grew. My hands dripped with blood and vibrated with a numbing pain. *Keep punching. Keep fighting. Keep striking. You're not done. Count, punch count, punch!*

Every prayer I had ever said screamed back at me with the overlapping voices. I heard a desperate young boy. I heard a devastated teenager. I hated God for doing this to me. I hated everyone for letting my life happen the way it did. I hated myself for not being strong enough to stop it.

I was battling my fears face to face for the first time in my life. My eyes streamed with tears, and my teeth ground together in anger. "You want to make something bad happen? Fuck you! Make it happen!" *Eight!* "I don't fucking care!" *Nine*! "I don't fucking care!" *Ten*! "You can... *Eleven*! "...kill me, I don't fucking..." *Twelve*! "...care! I'm done! I'm fucking done. Make it happen!" *Thirteen*!

I struck the wall with everything I had. *Fourteen!*

Fifteen!

I intentionally ended on a division of three, landing my last punch on a small mirror we had hung on the wall. I reached down for a shard of the broken glass, my hand nearly unable to grasp it from the swelling across my knuckles.

"Make something bad happen, I don't fucking care anymore! Fuck You!" I screamed in hysterical anguish.

I buried the glass in my skin and dragged it down my arms, across my stomach, and over my chest, again and again, cutting myself open with long thin lines. Why did they not see me? How the fuck did they not know what I was going through?

I saw my mother and stepfather smashing everything in the house. I heard their yelling, their screaming, and my mother's crying. Why didn't they ever hear mine? Why didn't they care? The glass slipped from my blood-soaked fingers. I fell to my knees and sobbed. Every muscle in my body stiffened with rage, resentment, anger, and desperation.

Do you see me now? This is how bad I hurt! This is how loud I scream! This is how hard I cry! Look at me now. Look at your son. Look at your brother. Look at your friend. Look at the boy, the teenager, the young man dying from the inside out. Do you see how bad I hurt now? Do you fucking see me?

Blood dripped down my skin from all directions and tears streamed over my face.

I collapsed, completely broken. I was beaten. Adversity, struggle, and destruction had won. The walls I had built to contain my true self now lay in rubble. The last of my strength poured out of me in streams of tears and blood. I had nothing left to give. I was empty, completely empty.

Dylan knelt next me on the floor as I lay shaking apart. "I understand," he said, rubbing his hand on my back. "It's going to be okay." His voice was calm, and he spoke straight from his heart. Over and over again he repeated, "It's going to be okay."

Later I called my mother and told her I needed

help. She brought me to the Emergency Psychiatric Center at the city hospital. After I spoke with them about my OCD and the rest of my issues, they determined the best place for me was a hospital in New Hampshire. They put me in an ambulance and drove me the two hours north to be admitted for an extended stay.

As I stood in the exam room, the door opened and another man came in. He had a neatly trimmed beard and wore a V-neck sweater vest that made him look trustworthy and kind. "Hi, Craig. I'm Bob," he said with a wide smile. His voice was caring and genuine. He extended his hand for an introductory shake.

I raised my arms up with a shameful expression showing him my hands were not in any condition to be shaken.

"Ouch," he said. "Looks like you did some damage there, buddy." His lighthearted tone instantly calmed the tension in the room. He pulled up a rolling chair and sat down, laying a clipboard in his lap. "Sorry to make you stand in your underwear like this, but we're all guys. It's just like the locker room, right?" His attempt to relate to me was well taken since the awkwardness of the situation had me very uncomfortable. I was fifteen years old, suffering from a nervous breakdown, and standing in my underwear with a social worker and a bouncer staring at me.

"Have you ever gotten a rental car, Craig?" he asked, obviously knowing by my age that I never had.

"No."

"Well, when you get a rental car they kind of walk around it before you drive off to take inventory of any dents and scratches that already exist. That way when you bring the car back, they can tell if you made any more damage than what was already there. You get it?" he asked with a quick wink and a nod.

I nodded with a clear expression of embarrassment.

He quickly turned the clipboard over and held it up to show me a sheet of paper with the outline of a human body. "Well, you're my rental car," he said.

His good nature was refreshing, and I found myself smiling for the first time since I could remember.

For the next three days I was put on suicide watch. I wasn't allowed to have any of my belongings or anything that I could potentially hurt myself with. They even took the laces off my shoes and the belt from my pants. I had to remain within the locked ward, in sight of at least one counselor, and I slept in the lobby in front of the nurses' station so they could keep an eye on me all night.

After the three days I was allowed to begin full-time treatment. I could leave the confines of the locked ward as long as I was escorted by a staff member. Still, I was required to remain on the top floor of the hospital. Although I did call my mother several times a day and begged to come home, the hospital wasn't that bad. It was well kept, and the staff was friendly and truly cared for the patients. They developed relationships with each kid and showed an incredible amount of tolerance for them.

The hospital had several wards, separated by age groups, adolescents and adults. I was in the adolescent ward with a dozen other kids all around my age. Despite the fact that we were all teenagers with different levels of issues, it was difficult for me to find a common ground with anyone. Most of the kids were there for behavioral problems. They were angry and threw temper tantrums to the point that their parents couldn't control them anymore. It was not uncommon to see someone throw a fit and get carried off to the "quiet room." A few kids had severe depression and two girls had eating disorders. But no one had OCD or the level of intrusive thoughts that I had. And none of the counselors were used to seeing my type of problems, either, except for Dr. Jacobs.

Dr. Jacobs specialized in OCD and behavioral therapy—a technique based on changing unwanted behavior by exposing the patient to triggers and then working with them to overcome the compulsions. He was a kind man with a warm smile. I took to him the minute he introduced himself. It was clear by my long hair and concert T-shirts that I loved music, and he started in on the topic right away.

"So you like music?"

"I do."

"What kind do you like?"

"It doesn't matter to me. I listen to it for the words, but I definitely like rock the best."

"I used to hang out with Aerosmith when I was a teenager, you know?" He used up our entire first session together telling me stories about high school and the days he hung around with Joe Perry and Steven Tyler before they were famous. He never once seemed condescending or that he was trying to work in a tactic of building trust with me. It was genuine. He had a glimmer in his eyes as if he had been waiting years to tell some of his stories and relive the moments for himself. After that, I looked forward to seeing him each day.

Our sessions were all based on behavioral therapy and challenging the dominant ritual behaviors associated with my compulsions. I had one compulsion that never allowed me to point a pencil in a specific direction when I set it down. I just spun it in circles for hours. The fear was that whichever direction the point was facing, something bad would happen there. So I could never point the tip toward myself or anyone else.

Once, we spent an entire session in his office working on this. He sat me in a chair in front of his desk and placed my hands on the arms of the chair. "Okay Craig, I want you to imagine that there are straps around your wrists and you cannot move." He offered to put real straps on me, but the thought didn't sit well with me. "I want you to fight this as hard as you can." He pulled two pencils from a cup on his desk and pointed one directly at me and the other directly at him.

I instantly broke out in sweats. He might as well have put my neck in a guillotine with a burning candle under the rope. I held out the best I could, but despite several future attempts, I was never able to last the entire hour.

In other therapy sessions he would dump out trash on the floor all around his office and make me stand there without trying to pick it up. But those compulsions were the easy ones to work on. Those were the ones you could see and feel. It was the compulsions in my mind that no one could get to.

Outside of the one-on-one sessions with doctors and counselors, I spent the rest of the time in group meetings. These were something to behold. They often began with strict agendas aimed at developing character and modifying social behavior. But someone would inevitably have a meltdown or refuse to participate, and the enthusiasm of the group leader would fizzle.

A couple weeks had passed and the end of my hospital stay was approaching. We had a group therapy session on the subject of showing emotion. About ten of us sat in a large circle. The room was set up like a hotel lobby. The chairs were cushioned with soft fabric and wooden armrests. Several small tables with ornate lamps were all around the room and generic landscape paintings hung on the walls.

James, our group leader, was a caring man who took

the time to get to know each of us during our stay. He always talked about his own kids, and it was obvious he had strong family values. He took a stack of index cards and spread them all out on the floor, in the center of the circle, facedown. "Okay, guys, we are going to go around the circle, and each person is going to pick a card. Each card has an emotion written on it: happy, sad, frustrated, etc. Once you get your card, do not show it to anybody. I want you to stand in the center of the circle and, without using any words, try to show us the emotion you picked. And all of us will try to guess what it is."

It started a bit awkward at first. A shy girl named Jenny, a bulimic, went first. She picked a card from the floor and stood in the center of the room clearly uncomfortable in the spotlight. She stood for about ten minutes not doing anything but playing with her hands and smiling uncomfortably with a red face while everyone called out their guesses.

"Shy!" "Withdrawn!" "Uncomfortable!"

Knowing this was going nowhere, James finally interrupted. "Okay, Jenny, we give up. What is it?"

She held up a card that read "frustrated."

"Ohh," James said, while furrowing his brow with a

gentle touch of sarcasm. "Sorry we didn't pick up on that."

We continued going around the room playing a game of emotional charades while each person picked a card and demonstrated it the best they could. I sat watching as each person got up for their turn and stood awkwardly in the center of the circle with a pouty expression or a big smile while we tried to guess what they were trying to show us.

The game dragged on forever. I began to feel intensely anxious as I counted the cards on the floor and performed compulsive rituals in my head. The air thickened with the passing minutes and it became increasingly harder to breath. The walls moved further inward and closed in around me. My knee twitched like a piston in a Formula 1 engine.

Emotional charades, are you fucking kidding me? This is ridiculous. How the hell is this going to make the numbers stop rattling off in my head or convince me that God wasn't going to destroy my life?

A boy stood in front of me rubbing his chin and looking to the ceiling. "Inquisitive," someone yelled out.

I had visions of my stepfather throwing me in the living-room chair and putting on cartoons to make me watch them. *Cry like a fucking baby.*

This whole game was childish. It meant nothing and was doing nothing. My neck beaded with sweat. My eyes darted across the floor. Scattered index cards became numbers in my mind. My chest constricted, and my skin felt tight against my own flesh. *What the fuck are we doing here? This is a goddamn joke!*

I reached down and took the card that was on the floor directly in front of me and turned it over. "*Anger*"

Anger! Fucking Anger! My self-control dissolved. The pages of a mental photo album flipped through my mind. A thousand pages passed for every second. And they stopped on the only visual representation of anger that I knew of: my mother.

The anxiety I felt over the last half hour exploded to the surface. I turned and picked up my chair and threw it against the door. I pulled the lamp from the table, ripped it from the wall socket and smashed it on the floor. I screamed and yelled incoherently. I envisioned my mother and stepfather tearing our house apart. I heard the sounds of shattering glass and pounding fists, and I felt the shockwaves of crashing TV's and furniture. *They broke apart my house! They broke apart my fucking home!*

The group ran to one corner of the room. I punched my fist into the wall and ripped down the paintings and landscape photographs. I wanted to keep going. I wanted to break everything in sight and let my emotions drain. I wanted to show each and every one of them what anger looked like. What rage really was. I wanted them to see it through the eyes of a boy hiding under his covers. *This is what anger fucking looks like. This is how you express an emotion.*

James came running over and tackled me in a bear hug. We both crashed to the floor. I lay with my head down on the carpet sobbing, my fists balled up and punching the floor. Thoughts of my mother's rampages pounded inside my head. James's grip turned from a restraining arm hold to a comforting hug as he felt me go limp on the carpet and curl into a ball like the little boy who hid under his covers with Winnie the Pooh. "It's okay, Craig. Let it out." He whispered softly, and rocked me back and forth to try and break me from my emotional trance.

I wanted to believe him. I wanted to believe that everything really was going to be okay. But no matter how much I cried, no matter how much I screamed and drove my fist into the floor, it would never be enough to make it okay. The pressure I lived with was so intense that not the punching, nor the screaming and wailing, nor even the lines of self-inflicted cuts across my skin, would be enough to let it all out.

+++++

The room closed in around me again. My breath was heavy, and my heart still pounded. I heard monitors beeping and alarms screaming.

My skin ran cold with the memory of cutting myself, and my fists throbbed from the remembrance of wild, desperately-destructive punches. There were so many moments when I had broken apart, and I seemed to remember them all through flashes of photographic images. One after another I saw them in my mind, and each one brought a sensation of emotional and physical release.

All at once, I felt a build-up of the desperate need to release my emotions. I felt pressure within me as if both my mind and body were expanding together. Then suddenly, like the exhale of a deep breath, relaxation came over me. I felt a sensation as though my body were slowly turning inside out. Release. Relax. Let go. I calmed. My heart steadied, and my breathing settled.

I was incredibly light and seemed to float in the midst of the darkness.

13 THE DREAM

I walked from the basement of my mother's house with a black trash bag over my shoulder and an overstuffed duffle bag in my hand. I took only what was left of my clothes and the few things that held any meaning to me. And though I never officially said I was moving out, it was obvious I would not be coming back.

It had been about a year since my hospital stay, and the tension in the house had grown to an all-time high. I was hardly at home anymore, staying at Dylan's as often as possible. My mother had enough issues of her own to deal with, so the added weight of mine was buckling her knees. A part of her actually needed it, though. I think it helped her to justify her own emotional instability. She would constantly talk with her friends and coworkers about everything I was going through-not in an effort to get it off her chest, but to make sure everyone knew that things were hard for her because of me. At least that's how it seemed. The intrusive thoughts, the medications, and the doctors were all openly discussed. When I called her at work, she would ask me how my symptoms were and what kind of day I had, and then loudly repeat everything I said for everyone in her office to hear.

Since I was now sixteen--the same age my brother Jay was when my mother kicked him out of the house-- things between my stepfather and me were worse than ever. He constantly gave me chores to do and forced me to help him remodel his house. His inspections were no different than they had been when I was a kid cleaning my bedroom, and he made sure to tell me everything I did wrong and then follow it up by calling me a half ass.

His years of torment had worn on me, and I had too many stresses of my own to worry about. Determined to save money for a car, I got a job at a grocery store. The struggle with OCD and depression had me under the constant threat of being fired. Between that and school, it was all I could do to keep myself together, and Steve was pulling at the threads of my splitting seams. It didn't take long for me to learn to shut him out completely. His words no longer had an effect on me, and I became really good at being able to deflect his comments. But this only made him angrier. He was pulling out his best weapons but none of them worked anymore.

One day he got home from work and sat me down in the kitchen. "We are going to have a talk," he said in a stern tone, as if he had been rehearsing the moment all day and was already worked up about it. He then started in with an angry rant. "Who the fuck do you think you are? This is my fucking house. As long as you're living under my roof, you will live by my fucking rules. Do you understand me? I will be respected in my house." He leaned forward, his voice grew loud and low, and he banged his fist on the table. "When I ask you to do something, you fucking do it."

I sat leaning back in my chair across the table from him, exaggerating a very calm, relaxed posture and said nothing. My lack of reaction enraged him. I wasn't fighting back or giving him valid reasons to get upset. "Do you fucking hear me?" he yelled, learning forward to get closer to my face.

"I will listen to you once you can talk to me like a human being," I said in an intentionally calm tone. "I'm not going to sit here while you scream in my face."

I stood up to leave. He jumped out of his chair and reached for me. "Sit the fuck down," he yelled, pushing his hands into my chest and grabbing my shirt in an effort to force me back to my seat. The feeling of his hands on my chest triggered a fire in me. My calm, passive demeanor shifted instantly to a protective rage. I swung my arms up, knocked his away, and pushed him back with everything I had. "Don't ever fucking touch me!" I yelled.

He tried to come at me just as fast as I had pushed him back, but I reached behind me and grabbed the kitchen chair I had been sitting on. I swung it up over the table, cracking him on the side of the head and body. I pushed him back again before the chair even hit the floor. "You don't ever fucking touch me!" I yelled again, and ran past him out of the house.

I didn't know where I would go once I left, but I just kept going, getting as far away as I could. I went to the place on the lake where Ally and I used to spend our days, hoping that she might be there waiting for me. I walked through the woods around the lake and eventually came to a clearing where the railroad tracks cut through our town. I walked along the tracks, breaking down inside. I thought of lying down across the rails and waiting for a train. I didn't know what to do. I couldn't go back to that house, but I had nowhere to go. Dylan lived more than twenty miles away, and I had no one in my town that I could stay with.

My walk took me all the way to the center of town where the tracks crossed over the streets. Dusk had set in and I was more distraught inside than when I first ran out of the house.

I looked down the street and saw Tracy, a girl I went to school with in front of her house. Standing next to her was Ally. They looked puzzled and surprised to see me coming from the tracks. I hadn't seen either one of them in quite some time, and I knew I didn't look good at all.

I walked over, my face worn with worry and exhaustion. I did my best to pull myself together. I wanted so badly for Ally to run toward me and tell me everything was going to be okay, but neither one of them said anything to me. They just looked concerned. "Can I use your phone Tracy?" I asked.

"Yeah...yeah no problem," she said, looking confused but too uncomfortable to ask what was wrong. I followed her inside and dialed my dad.

"Eden's." I recognized Carlo's voice right away.

"Is Bobby Miller there?"

"Bobbbyy!" he yelled through the noise of the busy bar. It was football season, and I could hear the game playing loudly over the crowd.

"Yeah, it's Bobby," my dad answered.

"Dad." The second I spoke, my eyes filled with tears and the weight of everything that had been on my mind came pouring out. I ran my sleeve across my eyes. "Dad, can you come get me? I need help. I need to get out of here."

Ally and Tracy stepped back to give me space. The situation was awkward and uncomfortable for all of us. I felt so embarrassed that I couldn't keep myself together. "I got in a fight with Steve, and things are really bad there. I need you to come get me, Dad, I can't go back." I wiped away my tears and tried to gather my composure for the sake of the girls, who were wide-eyed and whispering to each other.

"Ah, well... I don't know, pal... I uh... I don't know if I can make it out there tonight..." The noise of the crowd behind him erupted in cheers like someone had just scored a touchdown.

"Dad, please, I can't go back. I have nowhere to go."

"Yeah, uh, sorry, pal, I just can't make it there tonight. Why don't you see if you can stay with one of your buddies or something?" He sounded distracted as if his eyes were still on the TV screen and his mind was focused on the money he most likely had riding on the game.

"Okay," I said, standing up straight in an attempt to make myself strong enough to deflect that familiar disappointment he had made me feel my whole life. I knew that nothing I could say would convince him. I don't know why I had even bothered to call.

"Sorry, pal, take care."

I put down the phone, wiped my hands over my face, and took a deep breath. "I'm sorry, Tracy. Thanks for letting me use your phone." I walked outside and started heading back down the railroad tracks. I knew I had no choice but to go but back to my mother's house, and the thought of seeing Steve again killed me.

"Craig!" Ally came running up behind me. She had the look of genuine concern in her eyes. "Are you going to be okay?"

"Yeah, I'm fine," I said doing what I could to hide that I wasn't.

She reached out and put her arms around me, pulling me in. The smell of her hair brought me back to the summer days on the lake, and my heart fell weak with how badly I missed her.

More than a year had gone by since she had held me like that, and more than a year had passed since I had felt her touch. I wanted her to stay, to never let go, but I knew that things were still over between us. I knew that when she had left, she left for good, and this moment would soon be over, too.

She pulled back and looked at me, her eyes still as soft as I remembered. I turned away and walked back to my mother's house. God, I have to get out of here, I thought. This God forsaken town has nothing for me. I hated living with my mother and step-father and whenever I ran into Ally, or even heard her name, it broke my heart all over again.

It was late when I got home, and my mother met me at the door. She started giving me a familiar lecture about how I don't have to love Steve, but I do have to respect him. Steve had given her a very different account of what happened between us, and of course she believed him. Why wouldn't she? My mother had made it clear to me a long time ago that her husband comes first. She said it often: "My children are all going to grow up and move away someday, but my husband will be with me forever. I'm sorry, but he comes first." That was also her justification for kicking my brother out of the house when he was sixteen.

According to Steve's story, he had calmly explained to me how he felt. He was trying to help us find common ground when out of nowhere I started yelling about how I didn't care what he said. Then I threw a fit, broke the chair, and stormed out.

I didn't care what she believed. I didn't try to tell my side or stand up for myself. I couldn't, I had nothing left to give. Their house was a hostile cage, and the freedom and peace I felt at Dylan's place only accentuated how bad it was at my own. I had to get out. I made myself a promise that as soon as I got my own car I would drive away and never go back.

The next day after school, I took Dylan's bus home. We were up in the garage while Dylan sat on the floor strumming his guitar.

I sat across from him with my head buried in a notebook, writing a poem about wanting to leave home. I looked up. "What do you think is going to happen next?" I asked.

"I don't know, man. You can just stay here."

"No, I mean what's going to happen to life? Where do you think it is going to take us?"

"Who knows?" he said, looking off as if it was almost too much to think about.

"Do you think everything happens for a reason?" I asked.

"Maybe."

I stared at the wall across from me as if I were looking a million miles away. "When I was a little kid I wrote a note to God one night when my mother and step father were fighting. I left a big space at the end of the note and asked God to write me back, but when I checked it in the morning there was nothing there." Dylan continued strumming and listened intently to what I was saying. "But what was strange is that when I saw there was nothing there something told me to write in the space myself. It was like I was dreaming or something." My eyes darted back down to my notebook trying to snap myself out of the memory.

"What did you write?"

I ran my finger tip over the words I had been scribbling.

"To never forget how it felt."

"How what felt?" he asked with sincerity.

"Everything. Every moment that ever had an effect on me, I've always thought of that note--remember how it feels, don't lose it. Like there is some kind of purpose behind even the worst of it."

"Maybe there is." He strummed his guitar without any effort.

"What do you think it is?"

"I don't know." He shrugged.

I smiled and did my best to break the weight of the moment. "Maybe it's that guitar of yours and these damn words that keep jumping out of my head," I said, pointing to my notebook.

"Hey, better you scratch words in a book than scratch your friggin' skin," he joked, making light of my breakdown.

"Ohhhhh." I laughed. "Aren't you the expert, Dr. Dylan."

I knew Dylan understood me better than anyone, and over the next few months we openly shared everything. He saw the effect of the issues I was having at home, and he knew how I hated going back there.

I never actually told my mother I was moving out, and I never actually told Dylan I was going to live in his garage. It just sort of happened on its own, over time.

My work at the grocery store during the school year earned me enough money to buy a car. It was nothing special, but it ran well enough to help me keep my promise. Now, I was sixteen. I had my car, I had my license, and I was leaving.

I threw my bags in the backseat of my car and looked out into my mother's backyard. She sat on the deck and stared into a watered down glass of scotch. My stepfather walked through the yard and scouted areas of the lawn that were not up to par. I got in my car, backed out of the driveway, and pulled away. I never waved, I never said goodbye, and though we kept in touch, I never looked back.

+++++

I looked in the rearview mirror and watched the house fade in the distance. I had a dream to do something with my life, and I was determined to find my place. There was a nervous excitement in the fear of the unknown path ahead, but I had made my choice and was moving on.

As the images faded, the determination to continue down an unknown road remained within me. I had no idea what would happen next, how I would make it, or what life would bring, but I was moving on. I had an overwhelming feeling that there was something for me at the end of whatever it was that I was moving through.

I lay in the dark, overcome with the thought of continuing onward and leaving all that I could behind me. As I slowly fell back out, my fingertips rolled into my palms as if the steering wheel were still in my hands.

14 THE PEN

My fingertips were numb and weakened by the cold. It was all I could do to keep the pen in my hand and stare at a blank page in my notebook. It had been single digit temperatures for the last few days, and tonight was going to be the worst of the cold front. I shivered in the corner of the garage, wrapped in an old, dirty quilt with a broken space heater in front of me that I had found in someone's trash. It looked to be about twenty years old with a dented case and a perforated grate that protected a series of wires. Each wire hung loosely and flickered with a bright orange electric heat. The safety shut-off was broken, so the heater stayed on when it was tipped on its back, which made it perfect to cook on. I learned this one day when I sold my car for four hundred dollars just to get some money.

Things change fast when you're a teenager. My OCD had made it impossible for me to fulfill my responsibilities at the grocery store, and they fired me. I had outgrown most of the clothes that I took from my mother's house, so I desperately needed money. Selling my car was the best option. I went to the mall and bought some essentials: a pair of pants, a bag of socks, underwear, and deodorant. Up till then Dylan was letting me wear some of his clothes and sharing what he could, so having my own things again was incredible.

On the way home from the mall I passed the grocery store and couldn't help myself. I went in with a pocket full of cash and a stomach full of cravings. I left with everything from a box of fruit snacks to a big, thick New York sirloin. It wasn't until I got back to the garage that I realized I had no way to cook it. But when you're hungry, you would be amazed at the ingenuity you have and how well a twenty-year-old flickering space heater can cook a steak. After that I ate frozen pizza and burgers whenever I could get them.

Life in the garage had been anything but easy. I had no money, I had little food, and though Dylan's parents were aware I was spending a lot of time there, they didn't know I was actually living in an old barn out in the corner of their yard. Dylan would let me shower in the house and do some laundry while they were out. It was far from perfect, but to me, it was all worth it. It gave me the freedom to breathe a little and helped me to avoid the issues I had at my mother's house. The only downside was that the empty space those issues left had made more room for every other problem to grow.

Despite the daily doses of medication I took, the OCD continued to worsen, and the compulsions were constantly progressing into something different and more complex. My symptoms had progressed far beyond physical acts, like touching something a certain number of times, or flipping a light switch, to internal thoughts. Much like the numbers compulsion that forced me to count in my head, I had developed another one that forced me to reverse my words every time I spoke.

After each sentence I said, I paused briefly to say it backwards in my head. The idea was that my words could make something bad happen. I was putting comments and suggestions out into the world as I spoke out loud, and they could lead to something bad. The only way to prevent it was to take them back by saying them in reverse. The complexity involved in managing this, along with other simultaneous compulsions often overwhelmed me. With a lack of clinical support I developed my own self prescribed therapeutic plan: I cried my eyes out and wrote lyrical poetry.

School became a nightmare with all of this, and my already suffering grades flat lined. My guidance counselor had a pretty good idea of what I was going through. He took the time to talk with me often. He was a gentle man who seemed out of place in a high school filled with social tension, unruly students, and hardened teachers. He spoke softly and went out of his way to help me out. One morning, as I was walking down the hallway to get to my homeroom class, I passed him standing outside his office and he stopped me.

"Good morning, Craig," he said with a genuine smile. "Got a minute?" He brought me in his office and we sat down.

"How's it going?" he asked, obviously not using the phrase as a casual greeting.

"I'm all right," I said without looking up from the floor.

"Are you sure? Your teachers have been telling me that you've been walking out of class just about every day."

"It gets tough sometimes." I shook my head. "It's

crazy."

"Your thoughts?" he asked.

"Yeah, but that's just the start of it." I didn't want to talk about it with him, but I felt like I owed him the respect. He had been very kind to me all along. While I was in the hospital, the psychiatrists contacted my school and he was notified of my issues. "Sometimes I sit there in these classes, and I wonder what the hell I'm doing here."

"What do you mean, at this high school?"

"At any school. I don't belong here. It's not my place. I need to do something else with my life."

"Don't you think an education is going help you achieve that?" he asked, clearly trying to lead me down the right path.

"I can't even see a single number without spending an hour trying to reel my thoughts back in, let alone sit through an entire math class. I take more pills than I eat food. And I'm in therapy more often than other kids are at football practice. This isn't for me." I looked up from the floor and made eye contact with him. "There's got to be a reason for it. I've had a feeling in me for as long as I can remember that all this shit I go through is somehow going to be worth it someday. And I can tell you, this ain't it."

"What do you think *it* is?" he asked.

"I don't know." I shook my head and stared back at the floor. "I have no idea, but it's got to be something better than this."

He ran his hands over his legs, leaned back in his chair, and let out a deep breath. "Is that why you leave school all the time?"

"No, I leave school because I start going so crazy inside that I feel like I'm going to lose it, which I usually do right after I get out the door."

"I'll tell you what." He opened his desk drawer and pulled out a small pad of blank hall passes. He took a red pen from a cup on his desk and across the top of the paper, just above the words "Hall Pass" he wrote "PERMANENT" in big bold capital letters, then signed his name at the bottom. "I'll give you this if you promise to try and show up every day for school and do your best to stay all day. If you can't and you feel like you need to leave, then you can flash them this and just go, okay? That way it's official, and you're not just walking out."

I reached out and took the pass from him. He had the kind of smile on his face that was so sincere, I could feel it, and for a moment I felt as though someone understood me. He put out his hand to shake mine goodbye as if politely dismissing me, and I turned to leave.

"Craig," he said as I reached the door. "Just try to stick with it." He winked, and somehow I knew he wasn't just talking about school.

From that day on I did the best I could to try and stay at school for an entire day, but I rarely went to class. Instead, I stayed tucked away, hiding out in the back cubicle of the school's library, writing lyrics and poems. For some reason writing had become the only thing that was off limits to my OCD. When I was writing, I was free. I loved it for giving me that release. Some days I wrote ten or twenty pages of completely random things. One line after another, it didn't matter what it was about or even if it made sense. As long as the words were coming out, I felt okay. Sometimes I wrote poems, rhyming every line and using obscure metaphors to bury the true meaning. Other times I would sing a rhythm in my head and write lyrics that fit with it. When Dylan and I got home from school, we would sit for hours with his guitar, trying to make songs from them. I would sing him whatever it was that I wrote that day, and he would strum his guitar trying to find the perfect melody.

Writing became an obsession and probably the only healthy one I had. It not only gave me freedom from the intrusive thoughts, but it became my only outlet. It brought a new life to me as if I was tapping into a part of myself that was buried beneath my worry and depression. I wrote as often as I could, pouring out my deepest fears and purging the thoughts that were constantly polluting my mind. Writing separated me from my issues, even if only for the brief time that the pen was on the paper.

Some days I got so lost in a piece I was working on, I didn't remember writing it. Those were the pieces I loved the most. Those were the ones I kept with me always, folded up in my pocket and hidden away like prized possessions. When I felt overwhelmed, I would take them out and sing them to myself in an attempt to ease the pain. Sometimes the pieces I wrote stayed in my pocket for so long that the paper would become worn and fall apart in my hands.

But even more than the freedom from my illnesses and the release of my emotions, writing gave me something far more valuable. It gave me a sense of self-worth. It connected me with that part of myself that I always knew was in the background telling me it would be okay. I felt that little boy come back to life. The little boy who believed that God held the clouds still for him while he spun the world. And though I still suffered from depression, OCD, and anxiety, writing out the words made it so I was no longer suffering in silence. And singing them helped even more.

With Dylan and me playing music and writing songs all the time, the garage was becoming a teenage sanctuary. The broken front door, stuck in the open position, invited anyone who wanted to get away from their parents or be a part the music. People from high school and friends Dylan had known his whole life started to come over constantly, whether we wanted them to or not. It wasn't uncommon to have seven or eight people hanging around at once while we played songs and wrote music. Despite the company, however, I still felt alone. Other than Dylan, not many people could relate to my issues. And even at that, it was more like he just didn't judge me rather than he fully understood me.

The fact was, no matter how many friends came to hang out in the garage, at the end of the evening they all went home while I stayed. And this frozen winter night was no exception.

The wind circled the garage and howled as it pried its

way through the cracks in the walls. I sat back against the corner of the room with the space heater in front of me, trying to make the best use of it. I pulled the old, dirty quilt tightly around me. The cold air freely made its way under the blanket, where several holes had smoldered through from sleeping too close to the heater on nights before. The skin on my face was chapped with a cold, numbing burn, and my ears felt as though they might snap off. I leaned forward to get more light from the orange glow of the heater so I could see my notebook better.

My fingers were frozen and almost useless as I wrote, but I had to try. I needed to get this feeling out of me. Things had been hard lately. Depression hung on me like a shroud of lead, and thoughts of suicide plagued me constantly. I had spent weeks thinking of where I could go and how I could do it. It seemed so easy to just quit. But a part me still held strong to the belief that I had purpose. I couldn't bring myself to quit after coming this far. Everything had a reason and a purpose, even my own life; I just hadn't found it yet. But sometimes that philosophy got so hard to hold on to. Sometimes the world around me closed in, and all I could see was hopelessness in all directions.

The room was so cold, the night was so dark, and I was

so alone. I wrote in my notebook to the orange glow of the space heater while the cold continued to close in around me, and my heart absorbed into the page.

And now the pain sets in
With the cold of a dead winter wind
And all of the hope I had is gone
Covered in snow drifted thoughts

The footprints behind me all fade
With the words of the songs that I sang
That kept me alive through the nights
When reasons were so hard to find

Memories bleed from my scars
As I slip through the cracks in the dark
To a time when I wasn't so alone
When runaway thoughts would come home

And the fire that burned in my eyes
Was as bright as the stars I saw shine
As they led me along through the dark
And gave purpose for coming this far

But now the strength I gave to my hope
Lies frozen in words that I wrote
And the darkness murders my will
As the beat of my heart becomes still

And the embers fade out into gray
Taking the light of my faith
As I fall through the dark and the cold
While butterflies turn into crows

When I was done, I lay on the cold, hard floor, curled in a ball, and wrapped myself in a blanket full of holes. I pulled the space heater closer, shut my eyes to the thought of God, and whispered into the frozen winter night, "Please help me get through this."

+++++

The room closed in around me and became almost total darkness, but the flickering orange glow of the heater seemed to remain in my sight. I could still feel the cold bite at my skin while the heaviness of that night, and so many others just like it, thickened the air around me. I heard the faint sound of beeping and knew I wasn't in the garage, but I was too confused and too weak to try and understand.

I opened my eyes slightly for the first time. My lids felt like rusted metal doors, and my eyes stung with an acidic burn. I watched the ghostly orange glow come into focus, and I saw before me the blinking lights of a machine.

Cables ran from it in all directions, and I knew it was the source of the beeping I heard. For a brief instant I got a gray glimpse of a dark hospital room in the middle of the night. But it was all I could do to hold the focus. The heavy feeling of the lonely nights I had lived in a garage still clung to me, and when I saw the machine blinking a solemn orange light in the darkness of an empty hospital room, I again felt the heartbreaking loneliness I felt then and the desperate need to believe in something bigger than myself. My mind slowly spun in a warped, dizzying confusion-there is a reason, there is a purpose, God believes in me. I'm alive.

My eyes became heavy again as I drifted back out.

15 THE DREAM

I pressed the cold steel screen of a microphone against my lips. Dylan ran his palm along the volume knob of his guitar, and a low volcanic rumble shook the butterflies loose in my stomach. From behind me the drums crashed with an eruption of sound so powerful, it vibrated the stage beneath my feet. I took a deep breath and stepped into a brilliant white light. The silhouetted shapes of hands, heads, and arms swayed back and forth in the midst of the illumination.

The drums crashed again while the distorted static of Dylan's amplifier began to form a rhythmic wave of pressure and sound. I looked to the ceiling just as the lights rained down a carnival of multicolored hues over the entire stage.

My knuckles whitened by the grip I had on the microphone. I felt as though I were about to fall, as though I hung from the edge of a cliff, and the hard metal casing in my hand was the only thing left to save me. I needed this moment more than anything. For all of the fears that plagued me, being on stage wasn't one of them. Just as writing had given me the chance to get my words out, singing them gave me the opportunity to throw them out at full force. I never had a feeling or experience so powerful.

I stepped forward, closed my eyes, and began to pour out the words that had been marching through my head-words that for years had lain dormant on the pages of tattered notebooks or tightly folded away in my pocket.

I emptied my heart out, never truly acknowledging that I was on stage in front an entire club full of people. I let years of emotion drain as I sung about pain, fear, love, and heartache. I screamed from my soul and whispered from my heart. I even cried at times. My tears were disguised in the sweat that rained from my hair and dripped from my jaw.

We all had a passion that bled through the music: I, Dylan, and the others who helped us form our band. We were young kids just out of high school, ready to take on the world and present ourselves as we were, like it or not.

When the show was over, I was exhausted. I drove with Dylan back to the garage while carloads of friends and other band members followed us.

"That was unbelievable tonight," Dylan said. "You got a scream that people need to hear."

I slumped in the passenger seat with my head pressed against the window. "Better than the last one?"

"Better every time."

"I think we can make it even greater if we keep pushing ourselves," I said.

"We've only played half a dozen shows so far and look at how many people are showing up."

He was right. My self-doubt aside, I could almost say that things had taken off for us. We were rock stars in our own right. The garage had become a pseudo studio with amplifiers, speaker systems, and drums that lined the room. The walls were covered in sheets of carpet more than six layers thick to deaden the sound and keep us secluded from the neighborhood. And day or night, the room was usually filled with people who wanted a part of the action. Friends brought their friends who brought their friends. We took on a popularity like I had never experienced.

Some nights when people would show up to hear us practice we would play for hours while the room slowly filled with new faces, each person bringing whatever they wanted to party with: cases of beer, bottles of Tequila, and whatever drug they could get their hands on. By the end of the night the room was dense with a haze of pot smoke and the smell of spilled beer and stale cigarettes. Usually, there was at least one person who worked at a fast-food restaurant who brought leftovers from the night shift. We ate like kings when compared to cooking off the space heater.

In the morning the floor would be covered with sleeping bodies, empty beer cans, and burger wrappers. We usually woke to someone lighting a joint and passing it around the room while we argued over who was going to clean up the mess on the floor and the vomit on the stairs. Most of the time the room was such a mess, we used outdoor pushbrooms and snow shovels to clean up the floor.

For everything it was, though, we still had our innocence. We were naïve in our assumptions and lived only for the moment. Life was all about making music, shooting for the stars, and dreaming big dreams. But some were only there for the parties‑ new faces who had heard about the band and the studio party place.

"Yeah, it's definitely cool that we got all these people coming around, but, man, some of them are losers," I said, hoping Dylan would take some initiative and start being selective of whom he let come around the place.

"Don't worry about it."

That was always Dylan's answer for everything. Whenever a chance of something going sour propped up, I was always the one to see it coming. I was used to disappointment and knew what the bottom looked like. It was easy for me to spot it, and I was almost always right. But I think Dylan's deep fears made him unable to see anything negative. He was too afraid to worry and too afraid to consider consequences. He just brushed it over while trying to pretend that it would go away.

When we got back to the garage, the neighborhood was pitch black. Cars followed in like a small parade lining the street. Voices, laughter, and slamming car doors broke the silence. My head was throbbing. I was physically and emotionally drained. I had given everything I had that night on stage, and I needed to find a dark corner to collapse and be alone. Every night was a party like this and tonight I wanted nothing to do with it.

Dylan and I stepped from the car and began taking out all of our gear from the show to load it back in the garage. People whom I had never seen before walked past us, following others on their way upstairs.

"I'll be back," I said, setting down Dylan's guitar case on the ground.

"Where are you going?"

"I just got to take a walk."

I went about two blocks down the road to a concrete bridge that crossed over a small river. I jumped the guardrail and went down along the side to the water below. The moon filtered through the clouds and highlighted the river's movements. I was familiar with that spot. I had ended up there on Christmas a couple years before when Dylan's parents had a huge family party at their house.

I had sat alone in the garage, doing my best to not focus on the laughter and cheerful music coming from the house. But it was too much, and I had to get away. I tried to go for a walk that night, but I made it only as far as the bridge when a freezing winter rain soaked me to the core. I spent most of the night sitting under the bridge, waiting for the rain to stop and thinking about what Christmas would be like in my own house when I got older. I would have a real tree, a warm home with a fireplace and cinnamon candles. My kids would sleep safely and wake to a morning full of laughter and love.

I returned to that spot often, especially when the garage started to become more popular. It was the only place I could go to be alone. And it reminded me of the days when Ally and I would sit under the maple tree at the lake. Her arms around me, her hair trailing over my skin... I could almost still feel it, even as I sat alone on this night watching the moon gently lend its light to the surface of the water.

I spent almost two hours by the river's edge trying to regain my strength and pull myself from the heavy emotional outpouring I had at the show. I thought of the times when I first started to write, putting down anything that needed to come. I thought of the days when Dylan and I first started to make songs from it, alone in the garage with his guitar and my pocket full of poems. And I thought of the interviews I had seen on MTV of bands telling their story about how they made it big--days of being broke, partying constantly, and living only for the music. I dreamed of one day telling the same story in front of a camera: "The music happened on its own. It found us, and we just followed along."

Before I left to return to the garage, I looked back up at the moon as it hid behind a thin veil of clouds. The light barely broke through, making it appear as if God himself were somewhere behind the curtain.

When I got back to the garage, I could feel a low beating thud from the bottom of the stairs. I opened the door, broke the tight seal of soundproofing in the room, and was welcomed home with the blasting noise of a full-on backstage party. The music blared, joints passed from hand to hand, and burned-out cigarettes smoldered inside empty beer bottles.

"Miller, where the hell you been?" Dylan's voice cut through a crowd half made up of strangers. Some were passed out, leaning against amplifiers, while others huddled around a homemade bong surrounded in a billowing cloud of smoke. The sight of it got to me. It wasn't so much what everyone was doing, it was that they were all doing it in a place that I called home. To me, they didn't deserve to be there. They hadn't earned it.

I made my way through the crowd, bumping shoulders and cutting through conversations. I sat next to Dylan on what I had been using as my bed for the last few months--the backseat of a 1979 Blazer that had rusted out of a truck. It was like sleeping on a hammock after spending so long sleeping on the hard floor, even with the layers of duct tape that held the cracked, mustard-colored vinyl together.

Dylan was leaned back with the brim of his baseball hat pulled own over his eyes. His arms folded with a bottle of Coors Light in his hand. "Where the hell'd you go?" he slurred.

"Just took a walk."

"D'you write anything new?"

I looked around the room at a scene right out of a 1970's stoner movie and shook my head.

"I hate that kid," I said, pointing to a scruffy mess named Jefferson. He always had a look of deceitful worry about him like he had just robbed somebody.

"Youwa crazy tsonight," Dylan blurted. "People need tu hear thsat scream, Miller."

Dylan always had a way of getting me to break away

from whatever thought I was stuck on. I leaned back in the vinyl duct-taped seat. A hand came from beside me and held a lit joint in front of my face. I sighed, reached out for it, and pressed the warm paper and ash against my lips.

+++++

I felt the sensation of the warm paper pressed between my lips slowly turn into the soft synthetic rubber tube. I had an awareness of the moment. I remembered what it was like doing all the drugs I did and how I always dismissed the hesitation I felt just before I did them. I knew it wasn't right. I knew it would do nothing but hurt me and yet I did it anyway. I had a brief revelation of my self destructive behavior. I pressed my lips together again to feel the tube running over my lips. A feeling of shame came over me like I never knew before. What have I done? My God, what have I done?

16 THE SURRENDER

I walked the long driveway to Dylan's garage. I stared at the ground watching my dirty shoes kick up pebbles that spread out in front of me. My temples throbbed with pressure and my head hung heavy. I had just gotten back from a day of working odd jobs with a friend's father who owned a construction company. We had worked at several sites, but it was the final job of the day that tore into me. I wasn't prepared for it. Not in terms of the work required to complete it but in terms of the eye-opening effect it had on me.

About two years had passed since our band had started playing shows and though we were still stuck in the same place, life seemed to have moved faster than any of us could keep up with.

I hadn't done too badly for myself during that time- all things considered. For one thing, living on my own and surviving any way I could had taught me how to control my thoughts better. I had to; it became a necessity for survival. I was constantly battling depression and the intrusive thoughts of OCD, I was alone even when surrounded by friends. And I found myself very drawn to thoughts of suicide. Finding some kind of solid ground was crucial to moving forward.

I had put everything into making myself believe that music was my way out of it all. The lyrics and poems I wrote were the key to finding my purpose in life. It was the reason why everything happened. All the tragic events of my life were the ingredients needed to write great songs and help people identify with me the way I identified with the poets I read in the high-school library and the songwriters I fell asleep listening to every night.

Dylan and I had done well to bring our band to life and shoot for the stars. But when your dreams depend on other people to believe in them as much as you do, it is not always easy.

The garage was a notorious teenage night club, and what I had once called home became a dumping ground for every vagabond and drug addict in the city. It didn't take much for the real, serious drugs to break into our tight circle of friends, either. It started out as a onetime thing that we talked about for days after, joking about how messed we were and laughing about the crazy things we did. But then it happened again, and again, and the laughing stopped. It became less of a want and more of a need.

I would be lying if I said I wasn't part of it. I certainly wasn't a saint. I tried everything that was put in front of me but I never let myself get too out of control and I always kept my feet on the ground. I watched the people around me start to care less about making music and care more about getting high. The music became a distant second on the list of priorities with everyone, while I spent every day as a cheerleader trying to keep practice schedules and getting everyone together at the same time.

Even Dylan got swept up in it. He became so blinded by the veil of drugs that I didn't even know him anymore. And the friend who once believed in my dreams with me now stood by as they dissolved away, right in front of us. He even began to sell his music equipment to pay for his habit. It started with the small stuff: guitar pedals, cords and cables. Then he began selling off his collection of guitars. "All I need is one, Miller, don't worry."

But I did worry. The garage had grown so cold. Music was rarely played anymore, and our equipment was slowly disappearing. Every night was a full house with bodies laid out across the floor, packed together like a homeless shelter.

I don't know where it all went wrong. No single event changed everything, no move to a different town, no girl had broken my heart. A book of poetry hadn't triggered inspiration in me and drove changes in my life. A shift just happened on its own. Slowly, over time, I lost my hope. The darkness, the worry, and the fear that chased me my whole life had grown so widespread that even the distant spark of hope that told me to write a note to myself at six years old was no longer in sight. And I gave up on believing that everything had a reason.

The hardest part was that I felt it leaving. I felt my hope, dreams, and my belief slipping from my hands. I did everything I could to stop it. But the fact was, I lived in a garage no different than a back alley full of drug addicts. I had no money, no home, nothing of my own. I had to rely on everyone around me. I grew weak and angry. I hated myself for the way things had turned out in my life, and on this day, as I trudged up Dylan's driveway, it all came at me like a bullet to my heart.

That morning, when I agreed to work some maintenance jobs with my friend's father, I didn't know what was in store for me. The final job was at a three story apartment building in the inner city. When we arrived I learned that the top floor had been vacated... taken over by homeless drug addicts. The tenants on the first and second floor had complained, and our job was to build a blockade in the stairwell so no one could get up there anymore. The minute we pulled up I knew it was a bad idea.

People came from everywhere and surrounded us as soon as we arrived. With only three of us on the job, a truck full of tools might as well have been an open bank vault in that section of town. But we stayed and we worked, taking turns watching the truck. We planned for one of us to remain on the street while the other two went up and did the job. But first we had to make sure no one was inside the apartment before we blocked it off.

I went up with my friend's father to look while the other guy stayed with the truck, trying to fend off the hungry thieves. When I walked in, something just came over me. It was my wake-up call.

The place was a mess. The floor was covered in trash and make shift bedding. Dirty syringes lay strewn around and drug paraphernalia littered the entire place. What hit me most is that it looked so much like the garage. It looked like the place I called home. The thought sunk in me deep and weighed heavy on me the rest of the day. This road I was on was not taking me anywhere, and it killed me inside to think my life was such a waste.

My friend's father drove me back to Dylan's after work. For the whole ride home, I couldn't shake the feeling I had gotten from being up in that apartment. I thought of the garage and how much it had changed. Where there used to be guitar picks lying around, there were now rolling papers and pipes. Where there were once CD's of our favorite bands, there were now mirrors, razor blades, and even syringes. And where there used to be dreams of doing something with our lives, there was nothing but emptiness. It became so clear to me, and so ugly.

As I continued walking up Dylan's driveway kicking the pebbles in front of me, I couldn't shake it. I thought of how many times I made that walk and stepped into an old-decrepit garage on the verge of collapse. When I got closer to the door Dylan ran up behind me.

"Craig, wait!" he yelled out with an almost panicked concern. "I'm sorry, don't get pissed," he said, holding his hands up in front of him like he was surrendering at gunpoint.

For some reason, I had a sneaking suspicion as to why he didn't want me to go inside. I continued on and went upstairs. Dylan slowly followed behind, keeping his distance from me. I open the door, and what I found was nothing, absolutely nothing. Everything in the room was gone: guitars, amplifiers, songbooks, CD's, the drum set. *my* P.A. system, *my* microphones, and *my* cords, cables, stands, everything...gone-- sold for drugs.

I stepped into the room. I had never felt so devastated and invaded. Someone had snuck into my heart and stolen my dreams. Music was supposed to be my life. This was how I was going to make my horrible memories add up to something good. Writing lyrics and performing were the reasons for why everything had ever happened to me. It was supposed to be my answer. Now it was all gone.

I knew in my heart, though, that it had been gone for a while. It had been leaving one day at a time over the last couple years. But seeing the empty space made it so real. I circled the room in disbelief, kicking up pieces of trash that littered the floor: old pizza boxes, empty beer cans, and torn-up music magazines.

Dylan stood in the doorway and waited for my

reaction. In the corner of the room I picked up the blanket I had slept with for the last four years. It was filthy and covered with dark, smoldered burn holes from the space heater. On the floor beneath it was my notebook-- the only thing I had left. I picked up my notebook and walked over to the door to leave. Dylan stood uncomfortably in the doorway. His hair was disheveled, and his eyes were bloodshot. He sniffled and nervously scratched at his skin.

"I needed the money, man," he said as if desperately pleading for me to understand. "We'll get it all back."

I couldn't believe how bad he looked, and I couldn't believe I had let all of this happen right in front of me. "I don't care that you sold my stuff, Dylan. This place has been dead for a long time now, and if you don't take care of yourself, you'll be dead, too."

I walked down the stairs, across the collapsed floor and out the broken front door that had been stuck in the open position since the first day I entered.

The night quickly set in around me. Rain fell over me, dripped from my hair and soaked my clothes. I had no place to go. I was twenty years old, and the only possessions I had were the clothes I was wearing and a torn-up notebook. I was so burned out by life. I was angry and depressed. I fell deeper inside myself with every step I took, and the thought of ending it all seemed so easy. I continued walking deep into the night, finding my way onto the city train tracks.

A short length of the tracks cut through an area of woods and trees. It was dark and secluded. I followed the tracks in to the middle of wooded area. I could hear the cars as they drove over the wet city streets beyond the borders of the trees. I lay down over the rails. I had no real intention of killing myself, but I also didn't care if a train came or not. If it happens, it happens.

The back of my neck pressed across one of the cold, wet rails while my knees crossed over the other. I lay there in the dark. The rain fell through the canopy of trees and the smell of oil and steel filled the air. I closed my eyes.

"Hey!" A voice came from the darkness in the woods. I sat up to look, startled that someone was there. It was late, and raining, and I was in an area with no houses anywhere.

I heard them running toward me, and I jumped up.

"Jesus, buddy, I thought you were dead," a guy said, emerging from the woods and holding back a barking German Shepherd. "What the hell are you doing?" He was clearly shaken at seeing a body lying across the railroad tracks in the middle of the night. I was shaken myself as I thought of the coincidence of him being out there and finding me.

"Nothing," I said, "I'm all right." I wasn't about to confess my troubles to a stranger in the middle of the night. I walked away, heading back down the tracks that came out to a road. As I continued, I heard distant sirens wailing through the streets, and before I knew it I was surrounded with police cruisers. I stopped in the middle of the road. I had no reason to run and no reason to be worried. I knew why they were there.

"You okay, pal? Why don't you come here and talk with me for a minute?" one of the cops asked.

The lights flashed in my eyes. I was dizzy and so overwhelmed with everything that was on my mind.

"Do you have an I.D. on you, buddy?"

"No."

"You don't have *anything*?" he asked inquisitively.

His question struck me so much deeper than he intended. I stared ahead looking off into the blinding blue and white lights and my eyes began to fill. "No," I said...

"I don't have anything."

"Where do you live?"

Again, his question seemed to stab me.

"I don't know," I said with total honesty. "I don't know."

The moment seemed dreamlike, and I didn't even notice them calling for an ambulance. I just remember voluntarily crawling onto the gurney and being brought to the emergency psychiatric ward at the city hospital.

+++++

I hung in the moment. I felt the gurney beneath me and the dizzying moment of surrender that shrouded me that night. I lay in the dark, solemn and alone. The will to fight was so weak that I barely hung on to the moment of consciousness. The feeling of complete surrender engulfed me. I had nothing left. If there is a bottom, it was there that I lay. My faint awareness drifted again into a darkened void.

17 THE STRUGGLE

"Go sit down!" The psychiatric ward's strongest orderly stepped closer, his chest pushed out and his face inches from my nose. "You want to get hurt tonight?"

He hunched over and adjusted his head to try and make eye contact with me. But I continued to stare, counting the holes in the wire-mesh glass that protected the staff members from the patients. The nurses behind the glass looked like blurred blobs of color moving uncomfortably in the background, as if they assumed I was staring at them. He breathed heavily, with his fists clenched down at his side. He was ready. He wanted a fight tonight. They all did. They loved it.

Each ward in the state-hospital had at least one man

just like him. That was the protocol. They were big, strong, and knew how to take down even the most psychotic patients. They stood at the ready like soldiers waiting for the call to arms. If a patient was out of line they sounded a silent alarm, and each of them came from all over the hospital to wipe you out and lock you up. I had seen it happen all around me for days now. I watched them high-five each other after they pile drove a woman into the floor and dragged her kicking and screaming to the quiet room. I heard them laugh and joke about the man they took down the night before, how he screamed like a woman. And here I was, standing alone in the hallway, about to be their next story.

I said nothing and continued counting in my mind. I could not stop. I could not look away. I was fixated and under the complete power of my compulsions.

It had been about a week since the police picked me up from the train tracks and brought me to the hospital. And this was nothing like any hospital I had ever been to. It was cold and unwelcoming. The staff was heartless and cruel. On my day of admittance I stood in the hallway, and out of nowhere a man reached up from behind me. He grabbed me in a chokehold and dragged me backwards. I think I was too weak and distraught to care. I went limp and let him drag me down. When I hit the floor, he let go.

I stood and turned to find him laughing.

He was a patient with a crazy look in his eyes and a thick unkempt beard. "I was hoping you were going to turn around and kill me," he said. "You look like the kind of guy who would have fucked me up. I need a good ass kicking. Come on, man, just hit me a couple times?"

I knew then that I was not in a friendly New Hampshire "mental-health facility." I was in an outdated Massachusetts asylum.

I hated being there. Just the thought of everything in my life was too much to take, and this place made me feel even worse about myself. The same guy who begged me for an ass kicking ended up being my roommate. And he was more disturbed than I thought. Each night he would masturbate in his bed while pretending he was having sex with his mother and having a phantom conversation with her. It made things so much worse for me. My intrusive thoughts ran wild, and my OCD flared while I covered my head with my pillow trying to ignore where I was and what was happening.

The week went on, and I got more and more depressed. The doctor who was assigned to me was a hard woman who had worked for the state for years. She was the kind of person who believed everyone in there was psychotic. Anything you did to try and convince her otherwise made you look even crazier in her eyes.

She was on me all week, trying to dig the deepest dirt out of me that she could. She asked over and over again if I had been sexually abused as a child. I denied it until one day I finally gave in. I didn't care anymore. I was done hiding. How could things get worse? I went to her office, numb and ready. I was about to tell someone for the first time that I had been sexually abused for almost eight years of my life.

"Is there something you want to tell me?" she asked with a sarcastic grin as if she knew why I was there. She reminded me of a prosecutor who does everything possible to prove the guilt of the defendant.

"I was sexually abused when I was a kid," I said, letting out a deep breath, surprised that the words came out of my mouth.

"Hmmm," she said. "That. Is. Unfortunate." She clicked her pen and began writing in her notes as if I had just given her the one piece of evidence she had been waiting for.

"That's it?" I asked.

"Well, I figured you were," she said in a matter-of-fact tone and continued writing as if I weren't in the room.

"*Unfortunate?*" I leaned forward cranking my neck to try and get her to at least make eye contact with me. "Are you fucking kidding me?"

She stopped, raised her eyebrow, and set her pen down. "It *is* unfortunate that you were molested, and I'm glad you finally said something about it, but I think there is a lot more that you need to talk about if you are going to make any progress." She tilted her head and gave me a sarcastic glare. "Do you know what schizophrenia is, Craig?"

I nodded with firm-angry confusion.

"Are you aware that it runs in your family?"

"What?"

"Tell me, when you find yourself writing these poems--" she waved her hand in the air as if she were talking about a mythical, imaginary creature "--And you say that sometimes you don't remember writing them, what happens in those moments?"

"I don't know. I just get caught up in the moment." I shook my head and squinted my eyes.

"*Mmhmm*. Do you really think that God will hurt you?"

"No...what? I don't know." My frustration was building, and she saw it. I could feel her taking pride in her calm, sarcastic behavior as I was losing control.

"I think there is more here than you are aware of, and I will be recommending that you remain at the hospital until we can get things better under control." A cynical smirk pranced across her face.

"You can't keep me here."

"You don't have a permanent residence to go back to."

"I'll stay with my father."

"Do you think he will take you in?" She confidently batted back my comments as if enjoying the sight of the panic running through me.

"What the hell are you talking about? You can't keep me in here. Look at you, fucking smiling. I just told you I was molested, and now you're calling me schizophrenic and trying to fuck with me. You're crazier than any patient in this place."

She calmly looked down, clicked her pen, and began

writing again as if she had just gotten everything she needed. "If it is determined that you are a threat to either yourself or another person, then you will remain a patient here. Your hostility has me concerned." I left her office, and she never even looked up from her notes.

By that evening I was a mess. I wanted out of the hospital worse than ever. My mind reeled with old compulsions that I hadn't had in years. It was as if everything that had ever haunted me was rushing up from my past to attack me all at once. The confession of my molestation had brought up some of my deepest pain. I couldn't shake the visions and the feelings I had from it. I wondered if she were right, if maybe I was schizophrenic. Maybe I was worse than I thought. I never felt so heavy and so afraid.

That night I was escorted to the showers by two of the ward's orderlies along with several other male patients, including my roommate. The room had several shower heads spread out across two walls and a large drain in the middle of the floor.

We all showered while the two orderlies stood watching us, to make sure no one threw a tantrum and tried to hurt themselves or anyone else. I hated the feeling of it. Not only was I being watched as I showered, but I was showering with men. I thought of Jessica from third grade as she taunted me in the school yard. I looked over to see my roommate begin openly masturbating again and talking about his mother. The other guys ignored him and the orderlies snickered, but I couldn't stay there. I couldn't take it. I was getting sick to my stomach. I walked out and got dressed in a small changing area outside the showers.

Seeing the naked men in the shower brought me back to the days under the house and all the things Ben had done to me. My heart raced, anxiety rushed through my veins, and my chest felt like it was clamped in a vise. I was losing it, I was truly losing myself. My compulsive thoughts ran rampant through my mind like they had been locked away for years and were finally released from their cages. I walked down the hall. I wanted to go back to my room and bury my head under my pillow. I wanted to get out. I wanted everything to stop.

When I passed the nurses' station, that's when the wire grate that ran through the protective glass caught my eye and I began to count the holes in the pattern. I could not stop, and I could not walk away. I had to keep counting.

The nurses behind the glass had no idea what I was

doing. To them it appeared as if I was just standing there staring at them. They began nervously stepping away from the glass, but I had to keep counting. I had to keep doing it until it felt *right*, even with the threat of the ward's orderly rushing over to me.

"Sit the fuck down!" he yelled.

I ignored him and continued to stare, counting one hole at a time.

He stepped closer. "You're really looking to get hurt, aren't you?"

His chest puffed out and pressed against mine. But I had no intention to fight. I had no reason. I just wanted to be left alone. I just wanted them to let me count the holes in the grates of the window and satisfy the crazy, fucked up, ridiculous shit in my mind so I could go bury my head in a pillow and wait for the next day to come. But he wasn't letting up.

Suddenly, the door to the locked ward opened, and another half a dozen guys just like him came barreling in. The one in front of me pushed me back, and another one wrapped his arms around me from behind.

"Leave me the fuck alone!" I screamed. I tried to

break free but, he easily swung me off his hip and threw me to the floor. My body hit the shiny linoleum with a loud, hard slap and before I knew it they were all on top of me, twisting my arms back and working their thumbs into my pressure points.

"Leave me the fuck alone! Fuck you!" How dare they touch me? I was just doing my own thing. I wasn't bothering anyone. I fought to move, but they were on me so tight. My arms were bent back behind me, and several sets of hands gripped my wrists and ankles.

I hated them for targeting me. I hated them for targeting the others like me. I hated them for enjoying what they did and boasting about it. I wasn't going to be their next victim. I wasn't going to be their next story. I wasn't going down easy. I wasn't going to fold up, not without a fight. I had been folding up my whole life. I had lain down for everyone I ever knew to walk over me and step on me. I had been pounced on, victimized, and beaten down. But not anymore.

I wanted to fight. I wanted to bring them to the floor one at a time and twist them into pain and submission.

"Let me go, let me fucking go!" I screamed and yelled thrashing around like an animal caught in a net. I freed one of my arms and tried to pull it in front of my chest, but it was impossible. They had all their weight on me, driving their knees deep into my back and legs. I was pinned flat against the floor. I twisted and screamed. My head was turned and pressed hard against the linoleum as it raced with a million thoughts and emotions. "Let me fucking go!" I felt the trickle of spit running down the corners of my mouth as I screamed.

The pressure of their weight was so intense that every time I screamed, I lost a precious bit of air, and it became nearly impossible to inhale again under their weight. "Let me fucking go! Let me go. Let me go." I couldn't breathe. I had no room to fit any more air in my compressed lungs but still I tried to scream. I tried to fight. I tried to break free. But the oxygen in my lungs was exhausted and I felt myself quickly getting weak. I saw the room close in around me and a wave of intense dizziness as I started to pass out.

+++++

Everything went black. My head throbbed. The sounds of my screams echoed through the darkness, warping and twisting. I felt the weight of the men fade, but the pressure in my chest remained. I heard the intense screaming sounds of a heart monitor blaring like an emergency alarm. The pitch was so loud and so brilliant, it pierced my ears with a painful sting. I heard a breathing machine pumping in a rhythmic pattern that grew louder and louder crashing off the walls around me like a roman war drum. My ears were amplifying everything, turning every sound into a northeastern ocean storm pounding waves against the sides of my head.

I tried to reach up and cover them but my hands could not move. They were bound, tied, held down at my sides with what I knew were leather straps. They buried deep into my flesh with every movement and flex of my muscles. I kicked my legs and felt them on my ankles, digging into my skin. They were so tight, I thought my hands and feet were going to be severed. Pain attacked me from all angles. My body jumped outward with the overwhelming shock and intensity. I felt the IV's buried deep beneath my skin like poison daggers. I felt a fiery burn on the inside of my thigh and an extraordinary pain in the back of my head. The sounds were so loud, and the pain was so alive.

I twisted and reeled but was unable to move, unable to fight off the intensity of my senses while they peaked to their highest potential, desperately fighting to find life again.

From the darkness came a burst of light so intense, it seemed as though my pupils had dilated like telescopic lenses. The fluorescent lights became so bright they washed out all shape, color and dimension. The light burned through the skin of my eyelids as if I were staring into a hot July sun.

The reality of the moment flashed into my awareness. I knew I was in the hospital. I knew I had tried to commit suicide, and I knew I was alive, but why was I in so much pain? My suicide was an overdose, not a gunshot or a leap from a building. I had not thrown myself into traffic. Why did the back of my head hurt so badly? Why couldn't I see anything, and why was I tied to the bed? Confusion swirled within me, and panic crushed me in its grip. I began to see the moments of my life I had just relived in still, photographic images that flashed before me between the bursts of light and sound. My heart beat faster, and the monitor screamed at me. I wanted to cover my ears but my wrists burned with every movement. Please let me go. Please let me just cover my head.

I lay tied and defenseless as the onslaught of sensation attacked me from every possible angle and the vision of my life's most significant and painful memories repeatedly flashed before me. I felt everything all at once: the piercing sounds, the blinding lights, the sting of needles, and the grip of leather straps. I felt the fear, the panic, and the overwhelming desire to curl into a ball, put my arms around myself, and beg for it all to stop. I felt the pain in my head, the tubes down my throat, and a twisted knot in my stomach. God make it stop. Please make it stop.

I struggled and fought. I begged for it all to go away and still I was attacked. But in the midst of it all, while my body tightened and my mind spun in broken circles, I suddenly experienced a comfort in a way that I never had before.

As I lay fighting, struggling and confused while the relentless onslaught of sensation tortured my body, I felt the familiar warmth of my tears drip down the sides of my face. With the softest touch they poured over my skin as the only sensation that did not hurt. In the middle of my pain, of my death, of my struggle, in the middle of my life's most epic battle, all became still as the loving touch of my falling tears began to calm me. Each one kissed my cheeks as it washed over me. The pain and panic subsided. The images of my memories slowed, and I focused only on the tears that fell. Sounds quieted and light dimmed while love brushed over my cheeks. All went dark and slowly, through the comfort of my tears, my final vision came into focus.

18 THE VISION

In the darkness came a scene like none before. It was not a memory. It was not a photograph. It was like a movie played out before me. I was not the participant in this one but an observer. In my vision formed a room with a cracked window and yellowed shade that fluttered as the city's wind found its way into the room. A black ragged notebook lay on the floor with tear-stained pages and torn edges. I saw a nightstand made of milk crates and a rented bed with a borrowed pillow. And in it lay a young man who had just given his intent to die. I stared at him with such intensity and such insight. I did not see him as a man who had surrendered, I saw him as a boy who had survived. I saw him as a boy who lived some of life's most pivotal moments and experienced the painful beauty of human emotion.

I knew then as I stared at my own lifeless body on the bed that the memories I had just relived were not just memories but accomplishments. I felt an overwhelming knowledge that the events of my life had nothing to do with the names, faces, and details of the stories. It was what remained that mattered, it was the *feeling*. That is what propels us. That is what takes us forward and gives us new direction. The emotion that remains, the lessons learned, and the feelings that we take with us are all we need to continue.

The moment of my own death is what filtered out everything else that was not needed, everything I had carried with me for so long, buckling my knees and weighing down my will to carry on. It was a filter that trapped the shadows of doubt, pain, and fear, allowing only the light of hope to finally shine through unobstructed--the light I had known was always there.

In a grand shift of thought and perspective the moments that made up my life and who I was came together in a beautiful symphony of purpose, reason, and meaning.

I felt it resonate within me. I saw it so clearly with amazing perspective. I did not see a boy who hung from a fence scared to death while his mother screamed in anger and his brother whispered in reassurance. I saw a boy who learned that no matter how real our fear is there is always something there to remind us that it will be okay. I didn't see a boy trapped beneath the crawl space of his own house. I saw a boy who learned through the darkest of circumstances that compassion is to see the hurt in the eyes of another, no matter how badly we are hurt ourselves. I didn't see a teenager whose heart shattered on the side of a lake in the cold autumn air. I saw a teenager who learned from having touched the bottom of some of life's most devastating emotions that love, no matter how bad it hurts, is worth it. I saw a young man who learned from the crushing grip of mental illness that living within his own thoughts can be one of the most powerful paths to self-discovery. And I didn't see a man who wanted to die. I saw a man who had just given up on his dreams and beliefs.

In that moment, everything became so clear. I understood the power of experience and the incredible gifts they leave us with. I saw my life's events as badges of honor rather than painful memories. And it was then, as I realized that our memories are only valued on the imprint they leave, that I understood forgiveness- real forgiveness, not the kind that beckons you to look your assailant in the eyes and grant them pardon. It was the kind of forgiveness that takes us deep within our hearts, allows us to walk among the devastation and know that the pain had purpose, and that every scar and every broken piece is a seed that helps us grow. That is where true forgiveness lies: in the power to look at all the seemingly horrible things that have been done to us and not assign blame but instead give thanks for everything we have gained.

I watched. I stood staring at a man who lay quiet and hidden from the truth of his own life, a man who didn't really want to die but just wanted to be at peace. He had stopped listening to the voice that whispered it would be okay. He had forgotten, he had lost hope in purpose, and with it, he lost hope in his dreams. I vowed then never to lose hope again. Never let myself fall beneath the shadows of my own self-doubt and never, no matter how hard life gets, never to stop believing.

I floated, hovering in the darkness as the vision began to fade. My body felt enormous and vibrated at an extraordinary rate. And as I let the vision go, as I let it fade from sight, I held on to only the imprint that remained: the insight I had in my life's experiences, and the love I had for the man who thought his life was over.

+++++

In that moment, as I lay bound to the edges of a hospital bed in the intensive care unit, while machines breathed for me, and wires monitored what my brain could not, I had never felt a touch so beautiful, and so pure as the tears that fell from my eyes. I experienced a grace I had never known before and a touch so tender, it embraced my heart. The onslaught that attacked my body was over. All remained still and quiet as the tears continued their graceful, gentle touch over my skin. The battle was ending. Life had won.

19 THE SHIFT

"Mr. Miller? Mr. Miller, can you hear me?"

A nurse stood over me while I opened my eyes. I slowly gained focus and saw she was accompanied by two men in white coats who looked more like hospital bouncers than doctors.

"Mr. Miller, we are going to remove the tube from your nose." She spoke slowly, in a loud voice, as if she were speaking to a senile old man.

"You need to stay still for us. Can you do that?"

I leaned my head forward apprehensively, wondering why three people were there to take a tube out of my nose and why two of them looked like body-guards.

Before I could move, one man wrapped his hands around my head and forced it back into the pillows. The other man did the same with my shoulders. I jumped in a reflex reaction, only to find my hands and ankles still tied to the bed.

"We need you to take a deep breath and hold still for us, okay?" Her tone was somewhat degrading as if I wouldn't understand what she was saying.

She reached up, pulling the tube from my nose. I could feel it scraping the walls of my esophagus as she continued pulling. I gagged and tried to shake my head away, but the hands around me kept me still. She continued pulling the hose until I finally felt the end of it scrape along the top of my sinuses. I moaned and fought to reach for her hands again in an instinctual reaction to the pain, but the men pressed harder on my head and shoulders.

When they were through, they said nothing. The two men left the room while the nurse fidgeted with the buttons on one of the machines at my bedside. She turned off the breathing pump and scanned through a slip of paper that draped down onto the floor like a receipt from a register.

"How do you feel?" she asked, in a cold, formal voice.

"I don't feel good." My throat burned and my voice sounded hoarse and raw.

"I bet you don't. Sounds like your throat is sore, too. It will be for a while, but it will go away on its own. We needed to get your airway open because you weren't breathing on your own."

There was a distinct hint of disrespect in her voice as if I had wasted a lot of her time by being there. I suppose I didn't blame her, though. There she was, working all day to save the lives of people who want to live, and in comes a suicide victim taking her time and resources away from the truly sick.

"You're lucky to be alive, you know? If you hadn't thrown up whatever it was you drank, all those pills would have killed you."

It took me a second to realize what she was talking about. "I threw up?"

"You looked like you were covered in blood when they brought you in. What did you drink, cranberry juice or something?"

"Kool-Aid," I said. "Strawberry Kool-Aid." I thought

briefly about what she said. It surprised me to hear about something I didn't remember. I couldn't recall anything about throwing up.

"Why am I tied to the bed?"

"You were fighting us. Trying to punch at everybody and yelling out numbers. Do you remember any of that?"

"No. I'm sorry for anything I did, I don't remember." I was still too out of it to understand everything that was happening, but I knew enough to be ashamed and embarrassed for fighting them.

She ignored my reply and turned to walk from the room. "You're lucky to be alive, you know," she said again.

I closed my eyes. My head was dizzy and ached terribly. My body trembled with nausea. The pain in my thigh and the back of my head made it hard to concentrate and I felt like a bowling ball was slamming around in my brain.

A few minutes later, my father came in. I shook when I saw him as my shame and embarrassment became even stronger. He stared at me with a seriousness that gave him a stone-like appearance. He had a look of shock, concern, love, and anger all mixed into one.

"I thought you cut your throat," he said.

I stared at him, unable to understand what he was talking about.

"I went in your room to wake you up, and I thought you cut your throat." His eyes welled up, as he stared at the floor and tried to keep himself together.

I didn't know what to say. I pieced together the visual of throwing up the Kool-Aid and how the nurse said it looked like blood. I couldn't imagine what my father must have seen when he found me.

"I'm sorry." It was all I could think of to say.

"You need to take care of yourself." He stared at the floor. His hardened look kept the tears in his eyes from falling. He ran his hands down over his face as if wiping away any emotion that might be showing and left the room.

Throughout the day a lot of different people came in to talk to me: nurses and doctors checking me out physically, asking me questions about what kind of pills I took and how many. Psychiatrists came in and drilled me with psychoanalytical questions to determine my state of mind and if I was still a danger to myself.

By the afternoon I felt a lot better. They had removed my straps and most of the monitoring equipment from my body, and I was able to sit up in bed. I asked a nurse why the back of head felt like I had been hit with a bat and my inner thigh was burning so bad.

"We had to get blood from a main artery," she said. "We had problems getting what we needed from your leg, so we took it from your head." The thought of that sent shivers down my spine and made the pain feel even worse.

By the end of the day the doctors had determined that I was stable enough to leave the hospital, but the psychiatrists determined I wasn't stable enough to go home. Come morning, I would to be transferred to another institution.

20 THE BEGINNING

They discharged me the next afternoon and I was taken to the Brickman Hospital psychiatric ward just outside the city. I got a strange feeling from the moment I walked in. Brickman looked the same as any other hospital, but it felt very different. Maybe it was only the lingering effects of the last few days, but I felt the hospital had a dreamlike energy that made me feel calm and safe.

A staff member who introduced himself as John led me into the exam room to begin the admission process. He had light blond hair parted on the side and calm blue eyes that appeared gray up close. We were just outside a small common area on the ward set up with couches and chairs much like a living room. It was meant to make the patients feel more at home.

An African-American girl sat in one of the chairs with her shoulders hunched in and her hands pressed together between her knees. Her face was soft, and she seemed too young to be there. She stared at the floor with a sadness that seemed to be all around her. She was lost in an expression of detachment that made it seem like her sadness was not for herself but for those around her.

"That's Vanessa," John said, looking back over his shoulder as he unlocked the door.

I stood still for a moment, not realizing I was so impolitely staring at her.

"You'll meet her, don't worry." John put his hand on my shoulder and guided me in the room with him.

"So you've had a rough couple of days, I hear."

"Three."

"So what happened? You seem like a pretty solid guy. Did things just get to you?"

"Something like that." I was still thinking of Vanessa in the chair but quickly realized I needed to focus on the conversation. I followed up my reply. "Yeah, sorry I uh, I had some big problems for a long time, and I don't know…. I just decided to throw in the towel, I guess."

"What kind of problems did you have?" He leaned forward as though genuinely interested. His posture struck me. It had been a long time since anyone had taken an interest in my issues.

"It's a laundry list a mile long," I said, nervously looking down at my hands.

"Craig." He slouched and leaned farther in, trying to make eye contact with me. "I'm here to listen."

I looked at him for a moment, taken aback by his sincerity. I don't know what it was, but I felt like I should talk and tell him everything. He looked at me with a calming smile seeing that I was contemplating the thought of opening up.

"My shift just started, and you're not going anywhere for a while," he said with sly humor trying to coax me along.

"What do you want to know?" I asked.

"Everything."

I took a deep, slow breath, and prepared myself for

what I had never done. I talked. I told him everything. I told him about my mom and dad, my stepfather, about the incidents under the house. About how bad it hurt to have my heart broken. I continued for what felt like hours. He asked me questions about everything and left no room for gaps. I told him my most irrational thoughts, my conversations with God, my beliefs, and my dreams. I recited my poems and painted him a picture of the dilapidated garage that I once called home.

When I was done, everything seemed surreal. The calm feeling I had when I first walked into the hospital was now ten-fold. I felt light and free. And I felt safe.

"It sounds like you've been through a lot," he said "And look at you now, still healthy and still walking. Pretty impressive stuff."

He patted me on the back as we stood to leave, and I smiled politely unsure of how to accept his compliment. We left the room and I noticed Vanessa still sitting there, staring at the floor in the same position as hours before.

The next day everyone met for the morning meeting. A dozen or so patients and several staff members sat in a big circle in the pseudo living room. Some patients were still in their pajamas. The atmosphere was light and relaxed, and I felt more comfortable than I had in a long time.

One of the staff members, Donna, introduced me to the group. "Everyone, this is Craig. He just joined us yesterday evening, and he'll be spending some time with us." She was a sweet woman who spoke as if she were teaching a group of kindergarteners. "So anything we can do to make him feel welcome, let's do so. Why don't we start by going around the room and telling a little bit about ourselves?"

"I'll start!" one guy said, throwing up his hand. He was a portly man with gray hair and big, thick glasses. He had a permanent smile that made him look fun and lighthearted. "I'm Roger. I'm twenty-two years old and--"

"Garret!" Donna said as if she were trying to stop a child from being silly. The man and several others giggled.

"I'm just teasing," he said. "I'm Garret. I'm fifty years old, and I'm here because I'm crazy."

"Garret!" Donna said. "We don't say 'crazy' here, do we?"

Garret laughed and squirmed in his chair.

They continued to go around the room, introducing themselves one by one. Betty, an older woman, refused to give her age, but said suffered from depression and bipolar disorder. Kurt was there for a dual diagnosis: a combination of mental illness and chemical dependency. And Jack, a young man a little older than I in his mid-twenties, seemed to have a bit of a chip on his shoulder but in an innocent, pouty way. "I'm Jack," he said in a somber, flat tone. "I'm here because they won't let me leave."

I introduced myself. "I'm Craig. I have obsessive compulsive disorder and all the other things that go along with it."

"Oh, boy," Garret said. "This will be fun to watch!"

"Garret!" Donna said again, trying to tame his childlike behavior.

"Actually," I said with a grin, accepting his playful antics. "Most of my compulsions are all in my head, so there's not really much to see."

As we neared the end of the circle, Donna spoke up. "And this is Vanessa," she said, putting her hand on Vanessa's knee. "She's been with us for a little while now. She's a bit shy, but she can sing beautifully. Can't you

Vanessa?"

Vanessa sat in the chair holding the same position I had seen her in the day before. Her eyes never lifted off the floor while Donna spoke.

"I'm Donna," she continued, even though I knew who she was. "I'm a counselor with the hospital, and I also lead some of the groups that you will be attending. If there is anything you need, please let me or any other staff members know."

At breakfast I was setting up my tray as I moved through the line of a help-yourself buffet. I noticed Vanessa sitting quietly alone in the corner, eating a small plate of fruit. I got caught up again staring at her. There was something about her that I couldn't quite place. She looked so innocent and pure. She had smooth, flawless skin and a certain glow that seemed as if she wore her soul on the outside.

"She doesn't talk," Jack said from behind me. He still had that stern look about him that screamed an obvious front.

"Yeah," I said, intrigued as I continued fixated on her. "I noticed."

"I been here over a week now, and she's never said a word. Just walks up and down the hall all night singing the same damn song over and over, keeping half the place awake."

"What's that?" I asked, puzzled by his comment.

"You didn't hear her last night? She was walking down your end of the hall for hours. I could hear her all the way in my room."

"No, I didn't hear anything." I was still getting over the hospital stay in the ICU and had slept heavy.

"Well, you're lucky then. It drives me nuts."

Throughout the day I found myself inadvertently staring at Vanessa, hoping she would look up from the ground and say hello.

That night I awoke to the most incredible sound I had ever heard: a beautiful, angelic voice that resonated through the long hallway of the hospital with a serenity that seemed to comfort the night itself. I opened my eyes to see Vanessa's silhouette pass through the deep blue darkness of the hallway as she slowly walked by my door.

"Amazing Grace, how sweet the sound, that saved a wretch like me..."

Her voice was incredible- as soft and pure as she looked, and yet there was something so powerful behind it. I was overcome with a warm peacefulness that I had never felt before. I lay awake for nearly an hour listening to her sing *Amazing Grace* over and over as she slowly paced the hallway outside my door.

I thought of all the times I prayed as a boy. I had visions of nights in the garage when I lay frozen and alone on a hard wooden floor, asking God to help me make it through the night. I saw myself crying with my head in my hands completely empty of the strength to carry on. And I remembered lying my head to rest in the bed at my father's house, asking God to keep my soul

Her voice continued with an angelic sound that blended each word into one long, melodic, tone until I fell back asleep.

When I woke the next morning, I had forgotten for a moment that I was in a hospital.

The next few nights Vanessa continued to sing. Each night she paced the hallway outside my door as if she were delivering the words of *Amazing Grace* as a messenger for those who needed to hear them most. I lay in bed listening to her soothing voice and thinking about my life and how perfectly orchestrated each event seemed to me now.

A week went by. The hospital decided I was no longer a threat to myself, and they were preparing me for discharge. John had given me notice that on the last full day of a patient's stay, the counselors usually ask for a few parting words. I spent all morning thinking of something I could say to the group and jotting down some lines to myself, as I often did. Just after dinner we had our nightly group meeting, where we went around the room and talked about the day.

Garret told us a silly story about how he had a problem peeling his banana at breakfast, while everyone snickered. Jack told us with his hardened-flat tone about a plan he had been working on to try to escape. "You guys won't be able to hold me much longer," he said. And Vanessa looked at the floor and didn't make a sound.

When it got to me, Donna spoke up. "Craig, seeing you're leaving tomorrow, is there anything special you'd like to say? Maybe tell us what you've learned."

I stood from my chair and pulled a folded piece of paper from my pocket. I thought of all the days in high school when I kept my most important songs in there, keeping them safe like prized possessions. I remembered how much I loved the words for everything they had done for me and everything they had helped me get through. The room was quiet as if they could see my thoughts were temporarily elsewhere. I stood nervously unfolding the paper and began to read.

A morning snow fell just for me
And diamonds shined in yellow beams
I spun the world with my belief
But cried myself to sleep

I learned
It's through our tears we learn to see

In my darkest days, God showed his grace
Through a velvet veil of blood and pain
On grateful knees I fell to pray
But I was so afraid

I learned
It's in our fear we find our faith

Beneath a starlit sky and an earthly bed
We believed a promise had no end
She held my heart and took my breath
But "forever" died in autumn's death

I learned
It's a broken heart that knows love best

Words fell fast through a mind of holes
And filled my pockets full of poems
I took a chance and left the road
But I was so alone

I learned
It's the path we make that leads us home

Then there came a day when I'd fallen weak
And tied my hope from a hanging tree
I begged the lord my soul to keep
And fell to darkness in my sleep

I learned
It's in the dark we learn to dream

So when our eyes are set on the closing scene
Through the dust and haze we'll finally see
That the battles we thought claimed defeat
Waves the tattered flag of our beliefs

We will learn
It's the wars inside that bring us peace.

I folded the paper and put it safely back in my pocket. For a moment all was still and quiet. I started to sit back down, expecting Donna to give me a dissimilating thanks and move on to the next person. But instead everyone started clapping. I looked around as if I had missed something, but they were clapping for me! Jack stood up and his hardened glare appeared to soften. Garret yelled out that he wanted a copy of what I had just read, and Donna came over to give me a hug.

I was so taken aback I could not help but smile. I had never felt anything like that. I was astonished and incredibly proud. No one had ever taken an interest in my words. I felt a connection with each person who put their hands together in admiration for something that I had done. I felt like they understood me and they had seen me.

It was one of the most incredible feelings I ever had. In that moment I wasn't an outcast. I wasn't a failure or a bad student. I wasn't ignored. And I wasn't a "half ass." I was heard. I was seen. And I was being applauded for it. I looked around the room, scanning the circle flushed with pride, as they continued clapping. I saw Vanessa sitting motionless, still staring at the floor, but on her face she wore a smile as big as mine.

That night I hardly slept. The feeling I had from our meeting permeated me, and I buzzed with gratitude. In the darkness I heard Vanessa's voice soothing the walls that reverberated her words. I got up and moved to the door and saw her moving slowly in my direction. The dark blue hue of the dimly lit hallway seemed to glow around her silhouette. I wanted to talk with her so badly. I wanted to tell her how beautiful she sang and how she had made me forget I was even in a hospital. I wanted to make her feel as good as I felt when people applauded for me.

She moved closer. Her voice carried a harmony of notes that softened the night. "Amazing Grace, how sweet the sound, that save a wretch like me. I once was lost, but now am found. Was blind, but now I see."

She stopped in front of my door, fell silent, and lifted her head. She stared directly at me, and for the first time I saw her eyes. They reflected the dim light of the hallway like the stars in a midnight sky and had a depth as deep as her soul. I was stunned. For a week I had spent every day with her and never seen her lift her head, and here she was looking directly at me. I froze, forgetting everything I wanted to say. And before I could pull myself back together, she spoke. Her voice was so delicate but yet so serious.

"Did you hear them applaud for you today?"

"Yes," I said with a shy grin, recalling the moment and unable to hide my amazement at the entire situation.

She moved closer and took my hand. She held it with both of hers and lifted it to my chest. My heart fluttered with her touch. Her skin was softer than I had imagined. Her eyes peered deep into mine, and the night around us stood still.

"Don't ever forget how that feels," she said.

Chills ran down my spine, and my eyes welled up with astonishment. I thought of the note I had written to myself when I was six years old. I thought of that moment and how it made me know I was not alone. And I thought of how I had spent my entire life since then, absorbing my tragedies and hoping they would someday help me find my place.

I couldn't speak. I didn't know what to say. I was astounded with the entire moment, and my mind searched to make sense of the significance behind it. She brought my hand back down and gently let it go. I stood in awe as the night remained still. Her eyes dropped to the floor, and she slowly continued pacing the hall. Her voice picked up exactly where it left off.

"'Twas grace that taught my heart to fear, and grace my fears relieved. How precious did that grace appear, the hour I first believed."

I lay in bed the rest of the night while Vanessa's voice carried hope through the hospital hallway. The significance of what she said to me and the entire experience of the last two weeks overwhelmed me. My thoughts wandered through the memories I had relived in the Intensive Care Unit. I recalled the fights in my mother's house, the red-and-gold sign in the basement, and the move that took me out of the city. But it was my first memory that I couldn't shake- when I hung alone from a fence and fear had set the premise for my entire life. I was amazed I could so vividly remember a day from when I was so young. I saw myself at three years old, shaking and scared as my mother yelled and my brother tried to reassure me that everything would be okay. It was then that I recalled something I had previously forgotten: what happened next.

I sat in my bedroom as punishment and wasn't allowed outside for the rest of the day. I peered out a cold, frosted window all morning as the perfect layer of snow that blanketed the neighborhood slowly lost its magic. I watched the trucks drive down our street, plowing it aside and exposing the dirty gray cement. I watched my brothers shovel our walkways and pile it in mounds along the side. And I watched neighbors trample their feet over the sidewalks, peppering the smooth, white surface with footprints. I circled the floor of my room all day, dreaming I was outside tossing up the snow over my head, letting it fall around me like a real life snow globe, and kicking up my own path through an undisturbed canvas of white that had fallen just for me. I fell asleep that night to my three-year-old imagination dancing in a winter wonderland through my dreams.

When I woke the next morning, something amazing had happened. During the night, while I slept and my dreams took me away from the confines of my bedroom, it had snowed again. I pressed my forehead against the glass and looked out in amazement. The fear of my mother's wrath and the possibility of another punishment melted in the rising sun that sparkled across the surface of the snow. I quietly got dressed. I slipped on a pair of green rubber boots, and made sure my jacket was on correctly. I tiptoed past my mother's bedroom door, careful not to make a sound, and used a kitchen chair to reach the deadbolt. When I opened the door, the cold New England air gently brushed my face with a morning greeting.

I trudged down our walkway and up to the gate. I

climbed the snow pile against the fence. My anticipation grew. My brother's shoveling had made the pile so much bigger than it had been just a day before. I might be able to make it over this time, I thought.

At the top my feet were nearly as high as the fence. A cold wind blew the snow up around me, and the rising sun made it glisten in the winter air. I held my hand up over my eyes to shield the glare and wind, pretending I was on top of a mountain. I saw the road in front of my house covered in white and still not plowed. I saw the sidewalks free of footsteps, and I saw the pure white snow beneath me on the other side of the fence waiting for me to jump. My heart raced. I remembered how bad it hurt the day before, when I hung upside-down. I remembered how scared and alone I felt. But nothing was stopping me. I had waited long enough to get out there and I was not backing down.

I shuffled and stamped my feet into the top of the mound, making sure I had a solid platform to jump from. I bent my knees, got down low, and envisioned the powerful leap and a perfect landing. My hands shook, my heart pounded, and my stomach churned.

I closed my eyes, held my breath, and I jumped up with everything I had.

Time seemed to slow, and for a moment I felt as though I were suspended in mid-flight, caught between the fear of hanging helplessly alone and the belief that I would somehow be okay. With my arms spread wide and my eyes closed tight, I fell through the air and softly landed into the arms of a winter wonderland on the other side of the fence.

I raised my head and opened my eyes to the morning sun bursting out in all directions as it sparkled off the icy surface. And with the winter wind kissing my cheeks I reached down, took a handful of snow in each hand, and threw it into the air, believing in real-life snow globes and a blank canvas of white that had fallen just for me.

~This is How it Feels~

CRAIG A. MILLER

Authors Note

Following my release from the treatment center, I made a commitment to myself that if I was going to live, then I was going to *live*. I knew in my heart that I had finally begun to overcome the challenges that had plagued me my entire life. I focused my attention on learning everything I could from my past and using it to create a better future.

It has been nearly fifteen years since those three days in the Intensive Care Unit, and I still live with it as if it were yesterday, holding each lesson learned dear to my heart. I am now happily married and have two beautiful daughters. Though I have overcome the effects of OCD, anxiety, fear, and depression, I still write constantly. My mind races with words that want to escape, and more often than not, my pockets are still filled with poems held close like prized possessions.

The garage I once called home has been bulldozed to the ground. Dylan found refuge in a program that helped him get sober. Today he is a substance abuse counselor for the same program that helped him so many years ago. We meet when we can, and we still write songs together- my words and his guitar, the same way it started.

It took me some time to find the courage and to become grounded enough to write this book, but just like when I knew I was ready to move on with my life, I knew when I was ready to write my story. It is my hope to someday start a non-profit organization geared toward raising suicide awareness and prevention by encouraging the development of our passions, because I believe that it is in our passion that we find our purpose.

When the Cover's Closed

(2011)

Outlines of past lives silhouette my mind
Backlit with secrets and moments left behind
Of days when my heart bled, broken on my sleeve
And I stared off blinded in the brilliance of belief

For the words that came and the notes that played, I
have every song we sang
For the nights I prayed for a God to save, I have my heart,
my soul, my faith
For the memories and the sins in me, I have the ink
beneath my skin
And the dreams that left only emptiness, I have room for
what comes next

If you or someone you know is in crisis and needs help, please call **1-800-273-TALK (8255)** to talk to a counselor at a Lifeline crisis center near you.

Additional Resources:

Suicide Loss and Prevention-

- National Suicide Prevention Lifeline
  www.suicidepreventionlifeline.org/
  1-800-273-TALK (8255)

- American Foundation for Suicide Prevention
  www.afsp.org/
  1-888-333-AFSP (2377)

- American Association of Suicidology
  www.suicidology.org/home

Self Harm-

- www.selfinjury.com/

  1-800-DONTCUT® (1-800-366-8288)

Child Abuse-

- www.childhelp.org/

  1-800-4-A-CHILD (1-800-422-4453)

Drug and Alcohol Addiction-

- www.recoveryconnection.org

  1-888-705-2133

86738795R00163

Made in the USA
Columbia, SC
18 January 2018